World Party

Three Years to Change the World

Ronan Doyle

Concerned about the future of the planet, about climate change, conflict, poverty? World Party is your chance to create a new world vision

World Party

Three Years to Change the World

Ronan Doyle

ISBN: 978-1-84753-227-5

Contact the author at: ronanedoyle@hotmail.com

Preface

In 2007, it is clear that without radical intervention, the world is on course for catastrophe. This situation is man-made and arises primarily because our model of living in the West is unsustainable. Our actions have not only precipitated the current phenomenon of global warming, but by creating a society which is fundamentally dependent on inequality and injustice we have also been the catalyst for poverty and conflict across the globe.

Eight million people die needlessly every year because they are too poor to survive. In a world with abundant resources, 1.1 billion people live in extreme or absolute poverty (i.e. in households with an income of less than $1 a day and which cannot meet basic needs for survival). 75% of the world's population, or over 4.5 billion people, live impoverished lives on just 15% of the world's resources, while the rest (the West) gorge on the remaining 85%.

However, despite this obscene wealth, we in the West are not particularly happy with our lot. Increasingly, we are discovering that material wealth and consumption do not necessarily bring happiness and fulfilment. At the same time, we are also increasingly feeling insecure and vulnerable, because this unbalanced world we have created is now under threat. Climate change, global terrorism, nuclear proliferation and mass human poverty and suffering are just some of the symptoms that now confront us.

But it doesn't have to be like this. At any time, we the citizens of the West have at our disposal, should we choose to use it, the power to alter the course of the planet. As voters and as economic entities we have the capacity to realise a new vision of the world: to eradicate poverty, to halt climate change and to bring about global peace and reconciliation.

This book seeks to understand why, to date, we have not exercised this power. Why, apparently, we are prepared to allow our fellow citizens die in their millions every year, and why we stand by and allow the destruction of the planet, jeopardising not only our own existence, but also the future of our children and grandchildren.

Does the problem lie with our outdated system of governance, which is largely built around local and national structures, with limited global scope or accountability, and which is experiencing increasing difficulty in engaging with a disinterested public? Do we now need to develop a new "global" perspective and a new sense of "citizenship", which facilitates greater participation of ordinary people in shaping the world of the future.

World Party considers these issues and presents a proposal for a new innovative global project, initially lasting for a period of three years, aimed at developing citizen's awareness of global issues and coordinating citizen action across the globe to address these issues. People around the world would be invited to join the project, which, over the three year period, would aim to establish a framework for mass citizen education and action on key global issues (including climate change, poverty and conflict). This globally coordinated initiative would unite people around a common goal, thereby ensuring maximum impact and removing the sense of isolation and hopelessness that individuals sometimes feel in relation to their role in addressing global issues.

A global public that is informed, educated and that acts together in the interest of the planet and future generations is an unstoppable force. If, collectively, we can commit to such an initiative for a transition period of three years we will have already commenced our journey to the new world.

Contents

1 September 11

2 The end of innocence

3 Global citizenship

4 Think global, act local

5 Parents

6 Cultural leaders

7 The new world

8 Post materialism

9 The West's awake

10 The fall of the empire

11 People power

12 A new democracy

13 Losing our religion

14 World Party

15 A revolution

1. September 11

It was early May 2002 and my wife and I were returning home after a week's holiday in South West France. I remember it was one of those beautiful spring mornings, bright and sunny but with a slight chill in the air that gave everything a wonderful sense of clarity and freshness. Normally I felt quite subdued when returning from holidays but, helped by the weather I'm sure, on this occasion I was more upbeat than usual and I was actually looking forward to the flight back to Brussels.

It had been a wonderful holiday and as usually happens when a lovely time like this comes to an end and you're faced with the prospect of returning home, I began to take stock of my life – the bigger picture. What was the life I was returning to? Was I happy with this life? What kind of life did I really want? Was I fulfilling my potential and making my contribution to the world or was there something more? These were the kinds of questions that started coming into my head. Difficult soul searching questions that I had often asked myself before but never answered satisfactorily. But I was determined to keep asking them and for some reason, it felt like I might now be closer to finding some of the answers.

The idea of returning to the ordinary everyday drudgery frustrated me a bit. I had always believed that I had some sort of vocation in life and it frustrated me that I hadn't yet found it. In some ways I felt I was not living up to my potential. That I was merely treading water, waiting to spot the point to which I could swim with purpose, but in the meantime finding it difficult sometimes to stay afloat. I don't know why I felt like this, and I wasn't sure if other people felt the same way. I always presumed it had something to do with the fact that I probably displayed a certain promise as a child, which created an expectation that had lived with me ever since. Whatever the reasons, I had a certain expectation of myself, I felt that others had an expectation of me also, which I sometimes found burdensome. And now, at the age of 35, I was beginning to believe that I might never live up to this expectation.

I didn't exactly hate my life. It was just that I found little of purpose in it and I didn't feel I was doing what I should have been doing. I had a decent job that paid reasonably well. We had a nice house and a nice life in Brussels. But I was painfully aware that this wasn't everything, and yet, it really worried me that it just might be. So what would I do about it?

On that clear spring morning at 9,000 feet the world looked like a beautiful place. But the view was deceptive. In May 2002, it was pretty clear that the world had its problems. September 11 was still a vivid memory and, not surprisingly, weighed heavily on the public consciousness.

September 11 had sent shock waves around the world. It had left an indelible mark on everyone who had been around to experience it. In my lifetime, at least up to the present, it has undoubtedly been THE big event. I had always been intrigued by how people of my parent's generation would recall where they were when John F Kennedy was assassinated. Now I understood what they were talking about. You never forget where you are when you hear news like this.

For days and weeks after September 11 a grey cloud had hung over my world. It was as if someone had dimmed the lights and muffled the sound. It was a difficult time to be positive and hopeful. People were fearful and there was a gloomy feeling that things would never be the same again.

As the weeks and months went by a certain normality did return. But the seeds of change had been sown and a new vision of the world was already taking shape in the minds of men and women. An event of this magnitude and impact refuses to allow us to remain passive. It forces us to react, to take a stand, to change, to cry.

Something that intrigued me about September 11, however, was how differently people reacted. While there was, and rightly so, universal condemnation of the attackers and their tactics, it was encouraging that, for some people at least, it also inspired a more profound reflection. What had driven these people to carry out such a depraved act? How did we let this happen? Did we bring this on ourselves?

September 11 had been an act of desperate inhumanity and it was clear that there had to be something seriously wrong for people to perpetrate such a horrendous act. It was also likely that whatever drove these people to carry out this attack was likely to inspire further attacks in the future. It was imperative, therefore, that the world took a long hard look at itself and tried to figure out just what had gone wrong.

I, like many other Europeans and a sizeable number of Americans, believed that the US was at least partly responsible for September 11 (through its interference in the Middle East and elsewhere). But I knew that the US was not alone. All western countries were in some way complicit in bringing about this situation. The rich West enjoyed a standard of living that was beyond the wildest dreams of people in other regions of the world. The

West had been ruthless in its quest to achieve this wealth and superiority and it was equally ruthless in preserving it.

However, September 11 brought it home to me, and to many others, that our model for living in the West was fundamentally flawed. We could no longer go on ignoring the price the world was paying for our seemingly endless desire for greater and greater wealth. Western foreign policy was dictated by self interest, not fairness and humanity, although this was often the justification, and this was now coming back to haunt us. Ultimately, exploitation has its limits and on September 11, 2001 we were reminded, in the starkest possible terms, that these limits had been breached.

In the days after September 11, I began to realise that, despite what I and many other ordinary people felt, reflection and re-evaluation were not high on the agenda in Washington or London. Here the talk was of revenge and retribution and the tone was defensive. "Our grief has turned to anger, and anger to resolution. Whether we bring our enemies to justice, or bring justice to our enemies, justice will be done," President George W Bush told the US Congress on September 20th 2001. The message was clear, our way of life is right and how dare they attack it. We are right, they are wrong and we will fight to defend our way. "This country (the United States) will define our times, not be defined by them," declared President Bush.

Some kind of defiance was to be expected. I didn't really think that the US administration would suddenly admit that its foreign policy had all been a big mistake and that it was now going to mend its ways. I did, however, expect some signs of humility and some indication in the months that followed that the US might reassess its view of the world.

I was to be disappointed. The dangerous display of arrogance and self-righteousness that followed was horrifying. In its deliberations the US administration completely ignored the role of the West in creating the conditions that finally led to September 11, demonstrating it's unwillingness to recognise and confront its own culpability.

But it wasn't President Bush or his family that was paying the price for flawed Western foreign policy. In a speech to Congress after September 11, the President praised the real victims, and commended the bravery and heroism of the people who worked to the point of exhaustion to save the lives of their fellow citizens. He held aloft the police shield of a man named George Howard, who died at the World Trade Centre trying to save others. It had been given to him by Mr Howard's mother, Arlene, in memory of her son.

As is often the case in these situations, it was not the decision makers who were paying the price, but ordinary people like George Howard, or Todd Beamer (who lead the passenger takeover on United Airlines Flight 93 on September 11), who paid with their lives for the macho decision-making of the so-called political elite. It's heart wrenching to think of the suffering these people endured in their final moments, and the subsequent anguish of their families and friends.

Imagine how you would feel if it was your father or mother, brother or sister, or son or daughter who died in this way? Would you feel cheated, by the people who were took decisions that lead to such a situation? Would you feel angry, angry at yourself and the victims for allowing yourselves to be placed in such a perilous situation? Angry that you hadn't taken the time to understand what was happening and that you hadn't tried to do something about it.

As the flight continued towards Brussels it started to realise just how affected I was by what happened in the world and yet how ignorant and detached I was from it all. And it wasn't just me. Most people I knew were in this situation. Yes, we cared, and if we were pressed them on September

11 or on other global issues we had an opinion and we had ideas for how we would like the world to change. But mostly, however, these feelings and opinions remained dormant, as we got on with the routine of daily life. Any kind of active engagement on these issues was not really seen as an option. It was not part of our lives, like working or childrearing or sport. There was a feeling we had no influence over these things.

Countries were being invaded, our environment was being destroyed, and millions of people were dying of hunger and disease, but we just went about of lives without interfering because we felt we had no mechanism to "interfere." This though made me very uncomfortable and for the first time in a long time I realised I felt strongly, even passionately about something. Maybe there was something I had to do with my life after all.

2. The end of innocence

The day after our arrival back in Brussels I set up base in my newly converted office in a our Brussels townhouse. It wasn't very big, about 10 square metres, but it afforded me the time and space to begin to educate myself about the world and to better understand my own role as an ordinary citizen, and our collective role as ordinary citizens in influencing what happens in this world.

Picking up where I had left off the day before, my thoughts turned again to September 11. One of my abiding memories of this tragic event was how it revealed how much the direction of the world was out of step with what most ordinary people might have imagined or desired. It had taken us completely by surprise. Most people had never heard of Al-Qaeda or Osama bin Laden and they had never in their wildest dreams imagined that this kind of attack would happen, or indeed that there might have been any justification for it.

Sure, the media sometimes questioned the motives of US or Western interference in the affairs of the Middle East or elsewhere in the world. But for some reason, deep down we mostly believed that, despite certain indiscretions, our governments were by and large acting honourably and in our best interest.

Now, however, suddenly and sensationally, we realised just how much trust and indeed, how much power we had vested in our governments and how little we actually knew about what they were doing with this power.

September 11 was a wakeup call. Many countries had first hand experience of terrorism but no one had ever experienced a terrorist attack of this magnitude before, and with such indifference to the loss of civilian life. But once it happened, I, like many others, suddenly realised that maybe Western governance was not all I had imagined. There were things going on in the world that I was not privy to and they were important things; things that could change the course of our lives. It also dawned on me that, contrary to what I might have assumed, the West was vulnerable. The safety and security we had known all out lives could not be taken for granted.

The problem, however, was that people like me were waking up to this reality a little late in the day. Ignorance and blind faith had led us all into a false sense of security and now, suddenly, we found ourselves exposed and vulnerable.

The truth about the world we lived in was that the actions of the US and other Western countries in the Middle East, Africa, and also in Asia and South America were primarily driven by domestic economic and political ambition. Intervention in these areas was motivated by the need to ensure the supply of oil or other natural resources, or to open new markets for Western businesses.

There were, of course, also certain government-backed humanitarian initiatives, but these were often politically motivated or hampered by political concerns and were, therefore, invariably unfocused and fragmented. There was no serious commitment or ambition on the part of governments to alleviate or eradicate the problems of the third world. If there had been, much more progress would have been made.

Rather, the primary concern of Western governments was, and still is, to protect their own economic interests and to maintain economic growth and prosperity in their own countries. This is the holy grail of modern Western governance and is seen by the vast majority of mainstream politicians as the fountain of all political success.

However, before I go any further with lambasting politicians or apportioning blame to our governments, let me be clear. Ultimately I do not blame politicians or governments or business leaders for the predicament we now find ourselves in. The real culprits in all of this are me and you, the ordinary citizens. It is we who happily benefit from the economic spoils of Western policy and it is we who place it at the centre of successive domestic election campaigns. It is we who demand less taxes, more jobs, higher wages, and cheaper fuel. And it is we who continuously challenge our leaders to find ways to meet these demands.

We don't ask questions about how this is achieved, and we are generally happy to disregard the stories of injustices in far off places as exaggerated or outside the realm of our responsibility. Somehow, we seem to find solace in the fact that we are one step removed. Equally, while we don't ask our governments to limit aid to developing countries, we object vehemently to paying higher taxes or to accepting any erosion of public service provision in our own countries.

Politicians have always attempted to give us, the electorate, what they believe we want. Unfortunately, however, we have been selfish. We have failed to examine the consequences of our demands and the extent to which our political leaders have gone to meet them. We have been happy to reap the benefits whilst remaining politically ignorant of how this is achieved. In fact, it seems to be the case that the more prosperous we become the less and less interest we take in the politics of that prosperity.

Profit over Planet

The Nolan family had a successful furniture manufacturing business which they operated from a beautiful location in the Wicklow Mountains in Ireland. The business had been in the family for generations and, although it hadn't grown much it had always afforded the family a decent lifestyle. In recent years, however, the Nolans began to feel as if they were missing an opportunity. Benefiting from an upswing in the economy many of their friends and neighbours seemed to be making a lot of money. This was evident in the big new houses they were building and by the expensive new cars they were driving.

The Nolans, particularly the younger generation wanted a piece of this success and decided they were going to take action. At the next directors' meeting they put forward a proposal that the company should employ a "hot shot" manager to grow the business and make it more profitable. None of the family had studied business or had any international experience and they felt an outsider was needed to really aggressively grow the business. With the two older directors outvoted, the four younger Nolans easily won the 55% of the vote they needed to carry the proposal.

A few months later they employed John G. Clarke, a serial business achiever, who had started, built up and then sold no less than 5 successful businesses in the past 20 years. Clarke was a heavyweight and, naturally, he would have to be rewarded accordingly. But they were certain he had the wherewithal to take the business to a new level and that he would more than pay his way.

Clarke's brief was simple and that's how he liked it. His single instruction from the board of directors was to increase profits. At his first meeting with the board he was told that the business would have to become more profitable and that it was up to him how this could be achieved. As long as he delivered on profitability he had a free rein to decide on how the business should be run. In line with this he would receive generous bonuses based on a percentage of profits.

Clarke took up the challenge with gusto. In the first year, through a combination of cost cutting and the expansion of profitable lines he increased profits by 30%. In the second year he went even further and increased profits by a further 35%, again employing a similar strategy.

As the business grew and the profits rolled in the Nolans were happy to sit back and let Clarke get on with it. They were busy enjoying their newfound wealth and they had complete faith in him now that he was delivering what they wanted. Unfortunately, this was their cardinal error.

At first the problems seemed small and Clarke brushed them off as adjustment issues. Workers complained of the deterioration in working conditions, the freezing of wage increases, and the non-payment of overtime. Eventually, however, this unrest culminated with a threat of strike action, which Clarke dealt with by sacking the ringleaders and then by refusing to recognise the workers union. At this point things began to spiral out of control. Clarke's cost cutting was stepped up further and, in addition to wage and workload issues, workers were now very concerned that health and safety regulations were not being adhered to. Furthermore, rather than paying for proper disposal of waste materials, Clarke had instructed the workers to dump certain waste chemicals into a nearby stream and to bury solid waste on the grounds of the plant.

The concerns of the workers were privately raised with some of the Nolan family, who in turn raised them at a director meeting. But Clarke always shrugged them off, assuring them that everything was under control, that these were isolated incidents driven by a handful of disgruntled employees and that he was confident everything would be resolved satisfactorily. He also warned them that without ongoing change it would not be possible to continue to grow profits. The Nolans capitulated. The lure of further profits was too attractive. They might have had their doubts but they wanted too much to believe Clarke. The alternative was not a prospect they cherished.

The employees at the plant were in many cases longstanding neighbours of the Nolans and before long the family began to experience a certain coldness in the community. Their reputation as good employers was being compromised and their standing in the community was being damaged. The shopkeeper was no longer friendly, people avoided getting into conversation with them in the local pub and even their children began to suffer from verbal abuse and bullying at school. However, the Nolans had become very wealthy in recent years, they had bought bigger houses, bigger cars, and had developed much more expensive lifestyles. They had become accustomed to this wealth and they had come to depend on the profits of the company to sustain it.

However, things continued to deteriorate at the plant until eventually tragedy struck. A major fire broke out at the plant one night and three workers who were on a late shift lost their lives. An investigation following the incident concluded that all three workers would have escaped if the proscribed safety equipment had been in place. Because the company had failed to install and maintain proper safety equipment, as required by law, three lives had been lost, the factory had been burnt to the ground and, now, to make matters worse, because the correct procedures had not been followed the company's insurance policy was in question.

The company was faced not only with the costs of rebuilding and equipping the plant, but also with the compensation claims that would inevitably be lodged by the families of the victims, and which could run into millions of euros. In effect, the Nolan business faced financial ruin and it was the Nolan family, as the directors of the company, who were responsible. In fact, in addition to the financial crises they now faced, jail sentences were also possible if negligence was proven.

The business was in tatters and the good relations they once had with their neighbours and the local community was gone forever. And to compound their woes, the illegal disposal of waste into the local stream and on the grounds of the plant had also come to light following the fire.

The Nolans had made a fatal flaw in how they handled their business affairs and now they were paying the price. Firstly, they delegated responsibility to a manager without being clear on all aspects of what they wanted him to deliver (overly simplistic brief, driven only by profit), and secondly, they failed to monitor his activities and thereby failed to carry out their responsibilities as the company owners and directors. In the end, they paid the price as ultimately it was their business. They were the ones whose fortunes depended on the company and they were ultimately responsible for how it was run.

Managers, like governments, come and go. They are employed to do a job and to do this job successfully they need clear parameters and a well thought out brief. If their performance is measured on profits only, then their focus will be on profits only. If their performance is measured on profits, plus other issues, such as the environment, quality of life, external relations, then the focus shifts.

Managers, like governments, tend to have a short term focus. They generally look for quick returns and successes that will materialise during their term in office. They are less interested in what happens beyond this. Owners or citizens on the other hand have, or at least should have, a greater interest in the long term welfare of their business or their country or planet.

The reality, therefore, is that the interests of managers/governments and that of owners/citizens are not always aligned. Owners/citizens must, therefore, be aware of the issues affecting the long term welfare of their business/planet and they must ensure that these are adequately addressed by management/governments. The long term sustainability of their business/planet depends on it.

As the dominant living species on the planet we are the custodians of the earth and we have a collective responsibility for its care. Unfortunately, however, we have become negligent in our responsibilities. We have given political and business leaders the power to take decisions on our behalf and we have not taken the time or effort to learn and understand the implications of these decisions. The result of this is that we have allowed short term economic growth or "profit" to take precedence over the long term health of the planet.

The consequences of this situation are now becoming clear. Principally, we have adopted a model of living that is not sustainable. The Western world has developed a lavish lifestyle that is dependent on exploiting the resources of other regions and this is now causing untold poverty and social upheaval in these regions. In this context, September 11 was inevitable, and is likely to be just the tip of the iceberg. Further international terrorist attacks, environmental catastrophes, and mass human suffering through famine, poverty and disease are the unsettling prospects that now confront us. To anyone looking at the current status of the world with an objective and compassionate eye it is evident that the world must change course and quickly.

But how did this happen? How did we allow ourselves to be led down a road that was so obviously going to end in disaster? The answer in my view is very simple. Politicians know that citizens take a very parochial view of the world, despite the fact that politics and economics have now moved into the global arena. Citizens want jobs, lower taxes and at the same time good quality public services for themselves and their families, and politicians know that political survival depends on delivering on these key issues.

Politicians have, therefore, made this their raison d'être and have expertly exploited globalisation in an attempt to meet the needs of their electorate without ever considering or highlighting the wider consequences of their actions. Politicians have effectively put short term, parochial interests before long term social and environmental interests because this is what they rightly perceive to be the wishes of the electorate.

A better informed and more conscientious electorate might prioritise the need to ensure that economic growth is sustainable and does not impact negatively on the environment, or might demand that all members of society, including those living in developing countries, benefit equally and have equal access to welfare and justice. But this is certainly not the electorate that has been directing Western governments.

Of course from time to time a prominent scientist or famous rock star might draw our attention to social or environmental issues and, if the media give such events sufficient coverage, people generally respond. Unfortunately, this sentiment never appears to be sustained or accompanied by any genuine enlightenment of the population and there is no real commitment to addressing the root causes of the problem.

Too often it is a case of the musicians making music, the public making donations, the politicians making speeches, and then everyone going back to living as they always did, having cleared their conscience for another while and reinforced their belief that it's not really their responsibility.

When global issues are highlighted the public often blame politicians for not doing enough. At the same time, however, we also let them know that we are not prepared to suffer if something is to be done. We do not want tax increases and we do not want our relatively comfortable lives to be disturbed. In effect, politicians' hands are tied and to date, to the best of my knowledge, no Western politician has had the courage to really confront the public on this.

So how can we bring about the kind of radical change that is required to address this problem? It is certainly true that radical change is required. But I think the first thing that we must avoid is the association between radical change and radical protest. Radical change does not mean throwing bricks at police or shouting obscenities at world leaders.

Radical change, in my view, starts with a serious re-evaluation of how we live our own live and how we live up to our responsibilities as citizens. Taking radical action does not necessarily mean participating in anti-globalisation rallies or anti-war protests. And while some people might judge these actions to be justifiable and necessary a large proportion of the population consider this to be aggressive and confrontational and, therefore, tend to distance themselves from this type of behaviour and, by association, the causes they represent.

Because of this, such protests do provide a mechanism by which most ordinary people can develop a real understanding of global issues and their role in addressing these issues. Yet, real global change requires the support of these ordinary people, right across the world, and any attempt to bring about global change must, therefore, be open and accessible to such people.

Combating climate change, lifting Africa out of poverty, and bringing peace and security to the world requires the engagement of students, lawyers, doctors, entrepreneurs, factory workers, farmers and all people and professions that make up our society. We all have a role to play.

3. Global citizenship

One evening I was sitting my office, trying to find a few moments of respite from the stress and strain of life. But escape is not always easy in the modern world, especially when you live in major city, and the peaceful hideaway I was trying to create soon invaded by the commotion on the street outside. Through the window I could see people rushing hear and there, some were almost frantic, trying to find parking, rushing into shops, walking hurriedly along the street. And then there was a young woman in a red car, who was repeatedly beeping her horn at a car which had momentarily stopped in front of her to pick up two young kids. The pick up must have taken all of 30 seconds, but obviously this was 30 seconds too long. She was in a complete flap and showed absolutely no understanding for the man who was collecting his kids.

This incident is not uncommon on our streets today, but it brought home to me just how wrapped up we all are in our own little micro-worlds. In a way it is not surprising that we lack comprehension of global issues. If we find it difficult to try to understand the situation of the people in the car in front of us on the street, what chance do we have of understanding the situation of people who live thousands of miles away?

In the modern world we lead busy lives and all our time and energy seems to be taken up in dealing with our own everyday affairs. We seem to have little time or opportunity to learn about or reflect on global issues. In any event, we don't really see this as our domain. We might have some control over whether or not we have enough money to pay the mortgage or whether the neighbourhood is safe for our children, but what control do we have over climate change or poverty in Africa? Isn't this up to our governments?

This does seem to be the conventional wisdom, but is it correct? I don't believe it is and this, I believe is where we are failing as a society. This, in my view, is a fundamental weakness of the globalised world system of which we are now a part. It IS our domain and we DO have control over climate change, poverty in Africa and other global issues. The problem is, we have chosen not to exercise this control. Despite the globalisation of such concerns as trade, politics, the environment and security, as citizens we have remained parochial. We have failed to recognise our wider responsibilities in the globalised world and in so doing we have become powerless.

While I understand how this might have happened, and I am as guilty as anyone, I have more recently come to the realisation that this delegation of responsibilities is a luxury we can no longer afford. Public apathy and indifference to global issues have given political leaders the carte blanche to take us down the road to where we found ourselves on September 11th and to where we find ourselves today. This dereliction of duty is not a recipe for good governance and if long term solutions are to be found to the problems of the world then I believe the first step must be for ordinary people to forgo apathy and indifference and take on a new sense of global responsibility. We need to educate ourselves about the world's problems and we need to use our collective power as citizens, voters, and consumers to bring about a change of direction. We do have a choice and we do have the power.

If we want a better world for ourselves and for our children then we have to take responsibility for creating it. The priorities of politicians and business leaders are not necessarily a true reflection of what the priorities of a well informed and politically aware electorate might be. Politicians might enter politics with idealistic views about how to improve the world around them, but for (too) many, this is soon relegated to second place as career ambition or political survival take precedence. And when the public are not well informed and are unsure as to what they want, political leaders are very adept at filling the vacuum. If we, the people, don't have an agenda then the instinct of politicians is to substitute their own.

Today, perhaps more than ever, we need to have an agenda. Ordinary people urgently need to reflect on their role in the modern world. John F Kennedy famously challenged the American public of his generation when he called on them to, *"ask not what your country can do for you, but what you can do for your country"*. This was both insightful and provocative. It challenged Americans to rediscover their power as citizens and to use this power to make America a better place. In the age of globalisation perhaps it is appropriate that we now *ask not what the world can do for us, but what we can do for the world.*

A healthy democracy is one in which ordinary people are aware and active. Without this we have nothing more than autocracies, with the ruling elite deciding what is best for us (or them). The health of our modern democracies depends on the active and intelligent participation of all citizens.

It is true that in today's society a disproportionate amount of our time is either spent working or commuting or just dealing with everyday domestic issues. We seem to have no time to consider what kind of community we want, what kind of country we want, let alone what kind of world we want. But do we ever consider that this might in fact be a symptom rather than the cause of our disengagement. It doesn't have to be like this. Collectively we can demand time for civic duty or for other issues that we consider important. We can demand that working hours and commuting times are reduced and then challenge our governments to make it happen.

It is perfectly conceivable that we could reduce our time spent on certain activities (working, shopping, consuming, etc.) and absolutely critical that increase the amount of time we spend on others (family, civic responsibilities, etc.).

This, I believe, is a prerequisite to the development of a sustainable world. We must acknowledge that citizenship brings with it responsibilities and global citizenship brings with it global responsibilities. And if we are serious about building a sustainable future for ourselves and for our children then we must begin to take these responsibilities seriously.

> *"I am making a plea—a plea based on these ten years of looking at the human condition from my unique vantage point—for a dual allegiance. This implies an open acceptance of belonging—as in fact we all do—to the human race as well as to our local community or nation. I even believe that the mark of the truly educated and imaginative person facing the twenty-first century is that he feels himself to be a planetary citizen."* U Thant, United Nations Secretary General from 1961 to 1971.

4. Think global, act local

September 11th came as a terrible shock to everyone who was around to witness it. It was unexpected because most people were completely unaware of the context. Few people had much interest in or believed that they had any connection with or influence over what was happening in other parts of the world: in the Middle East, in Iraq, in North Korea or in Africa. Local and personal concerns were what really concerned most people. When will I get that salary increase I promised? How can I afford to buy the latest computer game for the kids? Wouldn't it be wonderful to have a holiday apartment in Spain? We really need a new car, especially now the neighbours just got one.

This preoccupation is understandable. These are issues that confront most of us on a day to day basis. There are also, however, other things that impact on our lives, often in a much more profound way that we rarely if ever consider. After all, what significance do holiday apartments or salary increases have to the people who died in the World Trade Centre or in the London Underground? What joy will new computer games bring to our children if the world they inherit is in crisis because of climate change and global conflict? How petty and selfish are our attempts to keep up with the neighbours if at the same time we completely ignore the plight of the millions of people dying every year from poverty and disease in the developing world?

In reality, we can't afford just to be concerned about domestic or personal issues. We also have a responsibility to be concerned about global issues and to use our influence as citizens to address such issues.

Take politics for example. Today, elections in most Western countries are won and lost and political reputations made or destroyed on the basis of domestic politics. And yet, international political decisions and agreements now have just as much, if not an even greater impact on all our lives than national or local political decisions. Indeed, this is reflected in the fact that a significant and increasing amount of our governments' resources are now also diverted to dealing with international issues.

Western governance is as much, if not more so about international politics as domestic politics because like it or not, we are now part of a global social, political and economic system and we are increasingly governed by international agreements on issues ranging from trade, to the environment, to security and health.

Some of the biggest decisions affecting our lives are now taken at international not national level, and appropriately in many cases. Climate change, air pollution and other global environmental problems do not respect national boundaries. Terrorism is no longer confined to regional or national conflicts. Trade between nations cannot be governed by national laws and regulations, but must be bound by international agreements and cooperation.

We have the Kyoto agreement on combating climate change; the World Trade Organisation (WTO) agreeing rules and regulation on international trade; the North Atlantic Treaty Organisation (NATO) to agree and promote measures for international security; and the World Health

Organisation (WHO) providing guidelines and direction on health related issues.

These international agreements impact on all aspects of our lives, from the creation of jobs and the viability of local businesses (farms, factories, shops, etc.), to the type and price of food and other products available in our shops and supermarkets, to the quality of the water we drink and the air we breath, and even to decisions on war and peace and on the very survival of the human race.

The problem, however, is that the people who represent us in this global governance system do really have a mandate to do so. We elect them to deal with domestic issues, not global ones, and as a result they tend to be largely preoccupied with the domestic rather than the global impacts of their deliberations. And given that the primary concern of the vast majority of politicians is political survival, then it follows that in international negotiations their prime concern will be to achieve what they consider to be the best outcome for their own constituency and not necessarily for the planet as a whole.

The result of this is that, while global governance is now becoming more commonplace and more influential in our lives, it is failing to address some of the most serious issues facing the planet. Success is largely confined to deals that deliver an immediate win-win for the negotiating parties while the more difficult issues, which sometimes involve sacrifices or concessions by certain countries in the interest of the greater good, get ignored or fudged.

It is for this reason that our modern global governance system is failing to tackle serious environmental problems, to address poverty and disease in the developing world and to eradicate the threat of war and terrorism.

Modern democratic governance has not embraced globalisation because when it comes to electing the people who govern our lives, decisions are still taken largely on domestic or local issues.

The most important questions we are not asking our politicians are: Will they contribute more aid to developing countries? What do they propose to do to try to address infant mortality and child poverty? Will they support tougher international measures to address environmental problems? How will they deal with international terrorism? We are not asking our politicians these questions and therefore their position on these issues is not a significant factor at election time. And yet, these are the issues that are critical to all our futures and that our political leaders are regularly taking decisions on in our names.

Politicians do not dwell on these questions at election time because the electorate are not demanding it. Why is this? How do we manage to detach ourselves from responsibility for what is happening in the wider world? Especially, when our actions and inactions have impacts far beyond our own national boundaries and likewise, when external actions and inaction have serious impacts on our own lives.

Would our governments do more to help the millions of people who are dying from starvation and poverty in developing countries if we the citizens and voters demanded it? Would the international community take more decisive action on climate change if we demanded it on the doorsteps during the next round of election campaigns? Would our governments continue to stand by and allow the clearing of hundreds of millions of hectares of rain forest every year if we made it a condition of our political support? And why is it that Islamic terrorists are waging war on the West? Is it because our governments are putting domestic interests first and are not being pressurised by their electorate to rise above domestic interests and engage in finding fair and balanced solutions to these international problems?

It is clear to me that the reason we are not being successful in tackling global problems is that we, the citizens, are not telling our governments to make these problems a priority. As citizens we have lost sight of our responsibilities to the wider community, to our fellow human beings and to future generations. If there is a solution to the world's problems then in my view, at its core is the need to recognise and accept this responsibility.

We are the ones with the power. We elect the politicians and we decide what issues should take priority. Equally, through our commercial actions and choices we decide who will be successful in business and what products and services they should provide. We hold the power, but unfortunately we give little thought to, and are sometimes irresponsible in how we use this power.

There are times when citizens need to direct their governments to take certain actions that they would not intuitively take. For example, there are occasions when a certain course of action is obviously in the global interest but might not necessarily be popular with a politician's local or domestic electorate. Political leaders will be slow, or even reluctant to act in these situations, unless of course they have clear direction and support from their electorate.

But such seemingly selfless action requires that the electorate has a sufficient level of awareness and understanding of global issues to recognise that action is required, and that they have the humanity to act in the greater good. I am confident that in the right circumstances people have the humanity. The problem, however, is that, in general, people do not have a sufficient level of awareness and understanding of the issues.

This, I believe, is a key factor in relation to government's inaction on key global issues. Doubling a country's contribution to overseas aid is unlikely to win any favours with an electorate that is ignorant of development issues, particularly if it is linked in any way to higher domestic taxes. Governments have everything to lose and very little to gain from such initiative. Yet, helping to alleviate poverty in developing countries is surely a moral responsibility and any citizen that is truly aware of the impoverished lives of millions of their fellow human beings would support this wholeheartedly.

Unless citizens demand action on global issues our governments will continue to pander to our domestic desires. It is clear, therefore, that the power to solve the problems of the world is very much in the hands of ordinary citizens and I believe that this power will only begin to be unleashed if:

1. citizens are properly educated about global issues
2. citizens in all countries, but most importantly in developed countries, demand that global issues become a top priority for their governments
3. citizens begin to take action in their own lives to give expression to their moral convictions
4. this citizen action is given professional guidance and support and coordinated at national and international level to ensure global impact.

In effect, in the global world in which we now live, we need to expand our concept of civic duty and responsibility and embrace the idea of a new "global citizenship"

Rethinking Democracy

Responsibility for the situation that led to September 11 and which will ultimately lead to further human tragedies can be directly attributable to our failing system of democracy. Governments elected for a 4 or 5 year term are required to "deliver" within that timeframe, which leads to short term and quick fix solutions. They are also required to "deliver" on the issues that most concern the constituency that elect them (tax, health, jobs..). In this situation there is little incentive to tackle difficult wider international issues that require a longterm outlook and that are not well understood by the electorate. This is a weakness of modern democracy. To overcome this we need a better informed electorate that demands action on global, as well as local and national issues, and that recognises and supports the efforts of governments to implement longterm sustainable strategies for the benefit of the entire planet.

5. Parents

Parents across the world have a key role to play in developing a new and more responsible attitude to global governance. No matter what race, religion, or creed, parents across the globe are united in their love for their children and in their desire to give them a hopeful future. This applies as much to parents in Iraq, Iran, Afghanistan, North Korea and Russia as it does to parents in the US or UK. No normal, loving parent would want to condemn their children to live in a world facing environmental catastrophe or a world ruled by terror and exploitation.

In this thought I believe there is hope. In the concept of parents and families, and the wider concept of community, I see the reason why people have historically sought order and security in the world and why they have striven and sacrificed to create and preserve this for thousands of years. I am also reminded of the song "Russians", by Sting, the lyrics of which are an important celebration of the potential power of parental love and an important source of inspiration for how this power can help us to overcome political shortcomings to create a better world.

In europe and america, there's a growing feeling of hysteria
Conditioned to respond to all the threats
In the rhetorical speeches of the soviets
Mr. krushchev said we will bury you
I don't subscribe to this point of view
It would be such an ignorant thing to do
If the russians love their children too

How can I save my little boy from oppenheimer's deadly toy
There is no monopoly in common sense
On either side of the political fence
We share the same biology
Regardless of ideology
Believe me when I say to you
I hope the russians love their children too

There is no historical precedent
To put the words in the mouth of the president
There's no such thing as a winnable war
It's a lie that we don't believe anymore
Mr. reagan says we will protect you
I don't subscribe to this point of view
Believe me when I say to you
I hope the russians love their children too

We share the same biology
Regardless of ideology
What might save us, me, and you
Is that the russians love their children too

This was a song of hope at a time when Cold War tensions were running high and there was a very real prospect of nuclear war. I was in my early teens when I first heard this song. At the time I was genuinely afraid that we were on the verge of World War III. Even as a young kid it was impossible not to be aware of the stories in the news or the adult conversations and whisperings.

This song helped me to see things from a different perspective. It helped me to realise two things. Firstly, I that they (the Russians, the perceived enemy) were ordinary people just like us, with children and families of their own. Why would they want to risk the lives of their sons and daughters any more than we would? And secondly, I realised that it wasn't just about Reagan or Krushchev, it was also very much about the people who gave them power. These were ordinary people, ordinary families, just like ours. Did these people really want a nuclear war?

Russian parents love their children. American parents love their children. Iranian parents love their children. Parents the world over love their children and it is these people, the parents of our future generations that must take leadership in charting a new course for the world. Ordinary people do not want to destroy the planet, whether by nuclear war or by global warming. Therefore, ordinary people have to ensure that it never happens. We have an opportunity now to overcome our misplaced cultural or nationalistic suspicions and perceptions and to be united in the desire to create a better world for all of our children.

Who wants to be around to see their children die from leukaemia, or the many other cancers and diseases, mostly attributable to environmental pollution, that are increasingly prevalent among the young and old? Who wants to see their children grow up in a world where the delicate balance of the world's natural ecosystem has been compromised? Who wants to see their children grow up in a world where more and more animal and plant species are becoming extinct, where rain forests are disappearing, and where soaring temperatures are causing mass human migration leading to widespread conflict and unrest? Who wants to witness the horror of another September 11, to see friends, family or fellow human beings trapped in a smoke filled room on the 110th floor of a towering inferno?

6. Cultural leaders

Undoubtedly, it is not always easy to sustain your commitment to global issues. The stress and strain of our everyday lives always weighs heavily. It is not always easy to find the time and the energy to educate oneself or take action on global issues. But I have come to realise that when I find myself in this situation I don't have to look very far to find inspiration.

Indeed, there were many such moments during the writing of this book. One evening, for example, I watched a documentary on television (BBC) about Victoria Beckham, former pop star and celebrity wife of the famous English footballer, David Beckham, spending time with a father and daughter in an impoverished village in South America.

The little girl, who appeared to be about 7 or 8, and her father spent their days scouring through rubbish tips searching for bits and pieces they could salvage and sell. On the day of filming they collected old animal bones and skulls, glass bottles and other bits of scrap, which they later sold for Stg£1.00. This would have been enough to feed both of them for a day, but on this particular occasion they decided instead to take a risk and invest the money. With the £1.00, they purchased a few rusty old barrels and a battered and rusted chair frame from a neighbour. They estimated that they could work this into a transportable shape and sell it on for a small profit.

Victoria Beckham, who was accompanying the two during their day's activities, was visibly shocked that they would consider spending their hard earned £1.00, on which they were dependent for survival, to buy what to her looked like complete rubbish. But they saw it differently, and later that day they sold this "rubbish" for £2.00, making a £1.00 profit on their investment.

Two things struck me about this film. Firstly, the almost unimaginable contrast between the lives of the girl and her father and that of Victoria Beckham. The father and daughter were lucky if they had £1.00 per day on which to live. Victoria Beckham's family income could be in the region of 100,000 times this, possibly a lot more. In other words, 100,000 families in this part of South America could survive on her family income.

But I was also struck by the contrast in terms of consumption and impact on the environment. This family had no material possessions (no car, no petrol consumption or emissions), they ate simple food that they produce locally, and besides the clothes they wore they had little else. They lived in a makeshift hut with no heating and no electricity. In effect, their impact on the environment could hardly have been lower, with almost zero energy consumption and close to zero waste / pollution production. In fact, by collecting and recycling waste from other sources (much of which originated in developed countries), they almost certainly neutralised whatever minor impact they did have on the environment.

By contrast, and without knowing very much about her lifestyle, Victoria Beckham undoubtedly drove one or several cars or SUVs, ate sophisticated meals (with food transported from all corners of the globe), had many wardrobes full of clothes and many rooms full of expensive possessions. And of course she lived in a super-deluxe mansion, with all the mod-cons: air conditioning, central heating, cinema screen, heated swimming pool, elaborate security systems, etc. In other words, Victoria Beckham and her family consumed vast quantities of the world's resources every day, produced vast amounts of pollution and waste and, generally, had a serious net negative impact on the environment.

Victoria Beckham might be an extreme case, but in reality this could have been anyone in the developed world. The shocking message for me in this piece of film was the sickening contrast between the lives of people in the West and the lives of people living in developing countries. In the West we consume resources at a rate which is unimaginable to most people in the developing world and as a direct consequence we produce vast amounts of waste and have a hugely negative impact on the global environment. If people in the developing countries consumed on the same scale and had the same impact, the earth would already be in tatters. *Western extravagance is, therefore, dependent on the impoverished and minimal impact lifestyle of the 75% of the world's population that live in developing countries.*

In this short piece of film it was evident that Victoria Beckam (representing the image of the West) enjoyed all the benefits the earth had to offer, while the poor family (image of developing countries) shouldered most of the responsibility. Victoria Beckham's lifestyle, whether she knew it or not, was dependent on their impoverished and low impact lifestyle. To be fair to her, she was trying to highlight their plight, which was nice, but who was she highlighting this for? She personally had the economic power to transform the lives of many thousands of these people, while at the same time reducing her own personal negative impact on the planet. If the film had ended with Victoria Beckham making some gesture of this nature then it would have been more powerful and even inspirational. But it didn't. She was highlighting the plight of these people but like the rest of us, she failed to make the connection with her own lifestyle. The same, of course, could be said for many other celebrities who use their status to highlight good causes. Don't just highlight the problem, lead by example, show us how we can all change our lives to overcome it.

Unless we in the developed world are prepared to do something about our own excessive consumption and waste production we will continue to be dependent on people in developing countries remaining as low consumers with no or very low waste production. In other words, we will continue to have a vested interest in maintaining the current imbalance. Therefore, if we are serious about finding solutions to the world's problems, poverty and sustainability must be addressed in parallel. And celebrities must take a leadership role in this. It is pointless highlighting problems of poverty and inequality while at the same time continuing to lead and glamourise a life of mass consumerism and wastefulness.

7. A new world

By nature I am an optimist. My natural instinct is to try to find the positives in everything and to try and turn adversity to advantage. This is also how I look at the problems I see in the world around me. Fortunately, the situation is not hopeless. If we act now, there is a very good chance that we can change things for the better. We can bring the world back from the brink and put it on a new and more sustainable course.

And think just for a moment where this could lead. What kind of new course we could chart and what kind of wonderful new world we could create.

I took the liberty of imagining what kind of world this might be, what kind of world I would like my children and grandchildren to inherit. It was a pleasant experience, which perhaps you could also try. In my vision of the world there was lots of green: green countryside, green luscious forests, and green towns and cities. A revelation in comparison to some of the grey and sterile places we know today. Life was less frantic. People worked less and therefore there was less traffic and less congestion, leaving more time, for other pursuits, such as leisure, learning, family and civic duty. The people living in these green places seemed relaxed and happy. It was as if that big dark cloud of pressure and stress and fear that we have all come to live with had been blown away. They were happy because they had learned to understand the world in which they lived and because they were now actively involved in changing it for the better. What I liked most about this visionary world, however, was how much richer people's lives were. And I don't mean material wealth. Materialism had all but disappeared in this new world, as people discovered more fulfilling and rewarding pursuits. Principle among these was their role as creators of a new world, a world in which materialism and consumerism were now seen as shallow, wasteful and ultimately, unfulfilling. People were no longer seen simply as economic entities. They now had defined roles as citizens, as family members and as individuals, and society had evolved to create the time and space for these multiple roles.

I was excited by this vision of the world, and while it was painfully clear to me that this was not the kind of world we were creating, I saw no reason why it couldn't be. Why should we not dare to imagine and strive for an alternative vision of the world?

Then I tried to imagine what kind of a world my children might inherit if things kept going as they were. Disturbingly, the very first image that came into my mind was from a TV programme about September 11 I had watched a few weeks earlier. It was an image of men and women trapped on the upper floors of the World Trade Centre. This was a horrific image of innocent people trapped in a living nightmare, with no escape and facing a slow, certain death. It was quite shocking, but I guess this image encapsulated for me one of the gloomy scenarios that await us if we continue on our present path. I also saw images of innocent young men and women struggling to survive in a world dogged with environmental problems and subsumed in conflict and instability. I saw how they tried to change things and how they wished we had acted earlier. But now it was too late. The damage had already been done. As I watched these heart-wrenching images of our children and grandchildren trapped in their "World Trade Centre," I regretted all the wasted chances and missed opportunities and I thought to myself, we can never let this happen.

The challenges are undoubtedly significant: the emerging threat of international terrorism; the ongoing proliferation of weapons of mass destruction, including nuclear weapons; the rapidly deteriorating state of our environment; the depletion of natural resources; the deepening divide between rich and poor. But now is the best opportunity we will ever have to address these challenges. The longer we wait, the worse the situation will get, until eventually, and in the not too distant future, we reach a point where it will be too late.

The magnitude of the problem we now face has begun to focus people's minds and in some ways it is one of those situations that had to get worse before it started to get better. It was probably always necessary that we would have to reach a crisis point before we would take action. Well, we have now reached that point, and we now have the option of doing nothing and living with the consequences, or seizing the opportunity to turn things around.

We have the potential to create a new world and we must derive hope and confidence from this. But hope and confidence alone is not enough, we must also take action and we must act together. Like Sting, I am hopeful because I know ordinary people around the world are decent moral people who love their children and want to see them inherit a healthy and habitable planet.

If the basic desires of these ordinary people can find expression and can be channelled into a coordinated citizen's response then I believe we can create an unstoppable force for good in the world. This, I believe, is the recipe for a solution and this, I believe, is the route to harnessing our considerable intelligence and creativity to build a new world.

8. Post materialism

I am convinced that the root of many of the world's problems is the futile obsession Western society now has with materialism. I am acutely aware of this because I am an active participant. Like everyone else trapped in this vicious cycle, I work hard to try to get ahead, to make enough money to buy a house and a car and to attain some financial security. And then, just when I think I have achieved all of this I find that society expects me to have a bigger car and a bigger house, and so I continue my quest to acquire possessions that I believe will demonstrate to the world that I have attained a certain status and, therefore, command a certain respect in society.

Too late into this game, however, we all inevitably discover that it is in fact never ending and that we are trapped. Not only do our materialistic pursuits command all our time and energy but they also drive us to become massive consumers and, consequently, massive producers of waste. The strange thing, however, is that while many people have the intelligence to realise how ridiculous this situation is, we seem to be powerless to do anything about it.

Up to a certain point, of course, materialism brings certain comforts (nice house, modern conveniences, car, etc.), which understandably everybody wants. However, beyond a certain point, which unquestionably many people in the developed world have reached, it seems to serve a different purpose. Beyond this point, materialism is about status and displaying the outward signs of success. The problem of course is that there is always someone more successful and, therefore, there is always something more to strive for. Enough is never enough. In truth, materialism and consumerism will never bring us the kind of happiness and fulfilment we think it will. Ask any rich person.

It is important, however, not to confuse materialism with wealth. In a free society it is inevitable that there will always be varying degrees of wealth. It is obviously preferable if wealth is not overly concentrated in the first place, but where it is it can be managed responsibly. Take Chuck Feeney, for example; a multi-billionaire businessman who could afford to live the life of an emperor. Despite his wealth, however, Mr Feeney owns no property, flies economy class, dresses off-the-peg and wears a $15 plastic watch.

In 1982, Mr Feeney founded Atlantic Philanthropies, which he has now given the task of giving away his vast fortune to designated charities before he dies.

Chuck Feeney is wealthy but not materialistic or ostentatious. He uses his money responsibly, not frivolously, which in my view does not make him any less interesting or influential than his counterparts. Clearly, it is possible to be wealthy and to derive satisfaction from one's wealth by using it constructively rather than destructively.

Chuck Feeney may be an extreme case in point, but this principle applies to all of us in the West. Last January, for example, I set myself the target of saving €10,000 by the end of the year. My initial idea was to put this money towards the purchase a car. To do our part for the environment, my wife and I have resisted buying a car for a number of years now, but it is difficult sometimes, especially when everyone you know has a car.

In truth, I know that we don't really need a car. We live in the centre of Brussels, less than two minutes walk from the nearest metro station, and whenever we need a car we can go to the car rental company down the road. But for some reason something keeps telling me we should have a car, everyone else does. The shallow little materialist inside me keeps asking me, how does it look to your friends, neighbours, family that you have no car?

But what if I decide to abandon the idea of buying a car? What if I decide to tell all these people that I don't have a car because I am concerned about the damage cars can do to the environment? What if I portray this as a positive thing and not something to be ashamed of? What if I decide that instead of buying a car that I'm going to spend this money in a constructive and responsible way? Perhaps I could invest €3,000 on installing solar panels on our roof in order to reduce our energy bill. Maybe I could also set aside €264 to sponsor a child in Africa for 12 months (€22 per month) and possibly donate a further €200 per month (€2400) to a self-help charity in Africa in whose work I could take an active interest, perhaps even volunteering some of my time. I could allocate an extra €100 per month (€1200) for our food bill so that we could buy locally produced organic food. I could also buy a new bicycle and still have some money left over.

For me, this would be a more rewarding way to use my money than putting it towards a car. I would get enormous satisfaction from knowing that part of our household energy requirement is coming from a natural and renewable source. It would also be very rewarding to be able to contribute something meaningful to charitable activities, and it would give me great pleasure to know that I am supporting the local organic food sector (food that does not have to be transported across the globe and the production of which does not damage the environment) and that I can provide more wholesome, healthy food for my family. And finally, my own health and wellbeing, as well as the health and wellbeing of the environment would benefit from my use of the bicycle.

You might have other ideas on what you could do if you were to free up some money, but the point is, we do have choices and responsible spending does not have to be less enjoyable or less rewarding; just more thoughtful. If people give greater consideration to the consequences of their expenditure then perhaps they would alter their spending habits. Through wiser and more responsible spending we can divert capital away from destructive and wasteful activities towards projects and activities that have a positive rather than a negative impact on our planet. As economic entities this gives us significant power. Collectively we have the spending power to alter the course of global economies.

Some might argue that spending and consumerism is necessary to sustain our economies and therefore to providing employment and to raising living standards. But it is important to remember that there is spending and there is spending. The production or provision of luxury goods and services, for example, takes valuable time and resources away from the production and provision of necessary goods and services. How many basic services (water, waste treatment, electricity, etc.) could be bought and made operational by engineers for the money and man hours that go into designing and building luxury pleasure boats or sports cars? How many children's lives could be saved with the money and medical resources that are now being diverted to cosmetic surgery?

Some people argue that it should not be a question of choosing one over the other, that we can do all of these things. This is clearly not the case, however. The reality is that while our consumption of luxury goods and services is at an all time high and rising, we are failing miserably in our responsibilities to provide for basic human needs in large parts of the world. We are failing to address poverty and human suffering, we are failing to maintain peace and security in the world, and we are failing to address the serious environmental problems that now threaten the planet. We have to get smarter and more equitable in how we use our wealth and resources.

Of course, it is also worth considering that there is more to life than the pursuit of material wealth. Making money has for many become the primary goal in life, often at the expense of the many other activities which are necessary for a balanced and healthy life, and which are fundamental to building a healthy and happy society. People are less active in their communities, they have less time for arts and culture, socialise less, and most significantly, do not have the time to understand and give effect to their responsibilities as citizens.

Materialism is defined in the Oxford dictionary as, "a tendency to consider material possessions and physical comfort as more important than spiritual values". Perhaps it is also time that we began to pay more attention to our spiritual values, but more on that later.

Materialism has become an integral part of western culture and cultural change can sometimes be a painful process. But cultures do change, and never has it been more important than now. To bring about such a profound cultural change require action on a number of fronts, not least of which is the emergence of leaders. The people who personify the image of Western culture are the celebrities: the film stars, rock stars, sport stars, high flying business tycoons, politicians, writers, etc. These are the people who have the power to lead a cultural revolution, and who better to help bring about a societal shift away from materialism than those who have helped to glamorise it in the first place? If they really care, as some do proclaim, these global icons can and should help to popularise a more sustainable and a more equitable lifestyle. And it's not enough for them to tell the rest of us what we should be doing. They must also do it, and be seen to be doing it themselves.

9. The West's awake

In the past few years rising oil prices have become a frequent news headlines. It seems that while supply issues have been partly to blame for this, a key factor has also been the rapid growth in demand. In particular, there has been much talk of the rapid growth in oil consumption in China and India, two big countries with rapidly growing economies.

China has been undergoing a socio-economic and political transformation for some years now. A key aspect of this has been the opening up of the Chinese market to world trade, which has helped China to achieve rapid economic growth in a relatively short timeframe. It is difficult to argue against this development, which undoubtedly has positive implications for the Chinese people. The problem, however, is that as the Chinese economy grows so too does its consumption of resources, and, as a consequence, its impact on the global environment.

China's consumption of oil is now growing at a rate of 6% to 7% per annum, which is not only putting additional pressure on global oil reserves, but is also adding significantly to atmospheric pollution, to global warming and to other forms of environmental pollution. What China is clearly demonstrating is that, as developing countries converge towards

Western standards of living, their consumption and waste production patterns also begin to converge.

This course of global development is unsustainable. The wasteful Western lifestyle may have been possible when only enjoyed by a small, privileged few, but the reality is that we cannot all live like this.

So how can the growth of developing economies be sustained without compromising the environment? Technology certainly has a role to play. Recent advances in the area of renewable energy production and energy efficiency are to be welcomed. Wind power, wave power, bioenergy, and in time, hydrogen power all give reason for hope. Unfortunately, however, the application of these technologies is still in its infancy and their potential to replace oil and other less environmentally friendly sources of energy is still uncertain, particularly in the context of surging energy demand.

For renewable energy to have any serious impact public policy would have to support the development and adoption of renewable technologies and practices on a much greater scale.

This would also, however, have to be accompanied by a serious change in lifestyles, with a significant reduction in consumption patterns. In the interest of environmental sustainability people might also have to pay a slightly higher price for renewable energy. However, this higher cost to households could easily be offset by savings accruing from lower energy consumption and improvements in energy efficiency. These measures must be developed in parallel.

It is worth remembering that consumption is a double-edged sword. In addition to the depletion of natural resources, our current model of global economic development also gives rise to serious environmental problems. We are now living with global warming, deforestation, loss of habitats and biodiversity, and a massive build-up of chemical waste and pollutants in the environment, many of which are now well established in the food chain and are known to be a major contributory factor to human health problems and to the huge increase in the types and incidences of cancers.

In 2003, the US Centres for Disease Control and Prevention published the National Report on Human Exposure to Environmental Chemicals, which was based on the largest-ever biomonitoring study conducted in the US. This study tested for and confirmed the presence of 116 different toxic chemicals in the blood and urine of a nationally representative group of Americans, all of which are linked to cancer and other defects and diseases in humans. One of the most disturbing findings of the study was that children had higher body burdens (levels of toxic chemical in the body) than adults of some of the most toxic chemicals, including lead, tobacco smoke and organophosphate pesticides. Most of the chemicals tested for did not even exist 75 years ago.

A question we must ask ourselves, therefore, is how long can the world go on like this? For how long can we continue to live in such a degenerating environment, where natural resources such as oil, gas, water, biodiversity, rain forests, and other natural resources are rapidly being depleted and where waste and pollutants are being accumulated at an equally rapid rate? For how long more will the world remain habitable?

It is possible that humans can continue to live with this situation for many generations to come, but as natural resources become scarcer and as the natural environment continues to deteriorate, as biodiversity is lost, as pollution and waste continue to accumulate, and as climate change accelerates and gives rise to more extreme weather patterns and to problems of erosion, flooding, drought and mass human migration, what kind of life would this be? And is this the kind of world we want our children and grandchildren to inherit?

Most people have some level of awareness of these problems and the serious challenges they pose. Unfortunately, however, it is a cause for concern that for the most part, people don't see themselves as being part of the problem and, therefore, they don't see themselves as being part of the solution either.

I often discuss environmental issues with friends and colleagues and a fairly typical view I hear expressed is: "How can I make a difference? I am just one person, what I do is certainly not going to change the world. And what's the point in me making sacrifices to try and save the universe when everyone else just carries on as normal? Why should I take the pain when they won't? Anyway, isn't it up to governments to sort out this problem? They need to sort it out. They need to bring in the necessary laws and regulations."

Certainly governments have an important role to play, but in my view the role of the individual is more fundamental. It is true that governments can bring in new laws and regulations. But think for a second what the public response might be. How would people respond to laws that might, for example, mean higher taxes on petrol and diesel in order to try to reduce fuel consumption, or higher electricity prices, higher water and waste charges, or that might mean tougher building restrictions? Laws that seek to control natural resource consumption or give greater protection to the environment could mean any number of measures that would be unpopular with the public. Governments don't like to introduce laws that make them unpopular and for this reason they have, to date, tended to avoid tackling these issues head-on.

The question that arises, therefore, is if governments are not prepared to bring forward and enforce legislation on these issues, how will they ever be tackled?

In my view, it comes back to ordinary people, but not acting alone, instead acting together and assuming collective responsibility. I believe that we need to orchestrate a collective citizen's response that facilitates local action but which is globally coordinated. Such an approach can provide a structured framework for action, which gives a defined role to ordinary people while at the same time removing the sense of isolation and hopelessness that typifies our sometimes individualistic view of the world.

An integral part of this collective, citizen-centred approach would be the education of the general public on global issues: to highlight global problems and explain the underlying issues, to demonstrate how the actions of ordinary people contribute to these problems, and to show how ordinary people can also contribute to the solutions.

If individuals and communities are assisted to educate themselves about these issues then I believe they will be encouraged and better prepared to take responsibility for addressing them. People have a moral obligation to do this, but they have yet to accept this obligation and their moral guides (parents, schools, the church, governments, etc.) have failed to properly promote it. Perhaps the opportunity now exists to do something about this.

Success in this endeavour, I believe, largely depends on three key factors. Firstly, people must see this as an opportunity. They have to believe that it is really possible to create a better world. I read in a recent edition of the Economist magazine that in a worldwide survey, more than half of the people interviewed believe that the world of their children would be a less attractive place to live. If that's the case, then why is half of the world's population not doing something about it?

Secondly, I believe that people must see the task of creating a fair and sustainable world as their moral responsibility, and this must be supported by those charged with moral guidance and teaching. In recent decades many people have turned their back on religion, which they see as having very little direct relevance to their everyday lives. These people have been left in a kind of spiritual limbo, with no organised and collective opportunity to reflect on their lives or on their moral values.

Surely, this is an opportunity to redress this and to provide an alternative route for individuals and communities, whether religious or not, to reflect on their role in helping to alleviate poverty and address environmental degradation and global instability. For those not currently aligned with any particular religious belief then perhaps this also offers a new opportunity for spiritual fulfilment. Our ancestors worshipped nature and the world around them as their God. Maybe we too can draw inspiration from this and rediscover our own spirituality through our relationship with the world around us.

Thirdly, I believe that those in positions of influence must show leadership. We don't need more celebrities telling us what to do; we need to see them doing it themselves. Highlighting issues is important and raising money is important, but it can't be a switch on switch off process. We need sustainability to become a permanent part of our lives and we need positive role models to lead the way.

In our communities, parents can also play a leadership role. Parents have a vested interest in the future. Parenthood transcends geographical, religious, and political boundaries. It can unite people from all walks of life and all corners of the globe in the common desire to create a better future for their children. Parents who want a better future for themselves and their children must take an active role in creating that future.

10. The fall of the empire

The US response to September 11 was pretty much what you might expect from a county big enough and powerful enough to win its arguments by force rather than persuasion. What's the point in getting mixed up in analysis and debate and compromise when you can just beat your enemies into your way of thinking with bombs and bullets. This approach is short sighted, however, and wholly inadequate when your enemies happen to be terrorists, capable of appearing and disappearing as the situation demands. A more appropriate response might have involved a somewhat greater level of introspection. If this had happened then it would undoubtedly have been a period of growth and learning for the US, which would, in my view, have seen it emerge stronger, safer and with its integrity intact.

Unfortunately, however, the US is not big on introspection and the decision to take the military option could, in my view, mark the beginning of the end of this modern day empire. I don't mean to be overly dramatic, but seems increasingly possible that September 11, while not fatal in itself, has drawn the US into a cycle of events that will eventually lead to its decline as a world force.

The invasions of Afghanistan and Iraq became the frontline of the US led response to September 11, the so-called "war on terror"; a war that continues to this day and which is potentially never ending. History has shown time and time again that terrorists are practically impossible to defeat militarily, and as an Irishman I am acutely aware of this.

In believing otherwise, President Bush and Prime Minister Blair ignore the lessons of Northern Ireland, the Basque Country, Chechnya, the Middle East and the many other regions of the world where terrorists have operated for decades and have yet to be defeated militarily.

If terrorists operating in such distinct geographical contexts cannot be defeated, how can such a diverse group of multinational terrorists operating across the globe be defeated? The reality is that the communities that breed the terrorists, and not the US President or British Prime Minister, will decide when this war ends. And that will only occur when the motivating factors that drive young men and women to join the ranks of the terrorist organisations and, importantly, makes this acceptable among moderates in their communities, are removed.

The emergence of this global terrorist network is a worrying development, and this type of conflict, which is not without precedent, has the potential to devastate Western civilisation. One only has to recall the great Roman Empire, which in its day was considered invincible in terms of its military, its technology, its governance and its sophisticated culture. But behind this superpower facade Rome was vulnerable, more vulnerable than anyone could have imagined, and once its vulnerability was exposed it literally crumbled overnight.

The Great Roman Empire, like our own great civilisation, was built as a matrix of highly interdependent activities. Viewed as a whole, this matrix seemed highly sophisticated and stable, but in reality it was extremely delicate and disruption to any one part of the matrix could destabilise the entire system.

The civilised and progressive lifestyle of the Romans was dependent on the great wealth of the empire, which afforded them the time and the money to make huge advances in areas of science and technology, commerce, art, public administration and governance. But Rome's wealth was largely derived from its conquests abroad and its capacity to exploit the resources and economic opportunities of its conquered territories. And of course, the success of Rome's conquests abroad was dependent on its powerful army.

But as the Great Roman Empire expanded across Europe and the Middle East it created a huge empire which was largely populated by dissidents. As the number of conquered territories increased, so too did the number of dissidents and, ultimately, the number of people plotting its downfall. Eventually, the Empire reached its limits as the Roman armies become overstretched. Rome had peaked and at this moment, and to its peril, it discovered the challenge of trying to temper the expectations and ambitions of a people who had been conditioned for growth and expansion.

Men and their capital are drawn to growth and opportunity and Rome could no longer offer this. So instead of the long period of stagnation or slow decline that one might have predicted, Rome went into a period of rapid decline. With its armies overstretched and its coffers depleted, Roman became increasingly vulnerable to attacks from its enemies. Rome then experienced the mobility of resources as its wealthy and educated citizens went looking for opportunities elsewhere.

The parallels with our own modern civilisation and with the US in particular are obvious. Like the latter day Roman Empire, the US is the world's modern superpower. It has extensive economic interests across the globe and has the military might to expand and protect its interest, anywhere, anytime. Like Roman, the US and its Western allies have used their economic and military superiority to exploit the riches of many other regions of the world and in doing so have made many enemies.

Further opportunities for expansion of US interests across the globe are now limited, thereby limiting future growth prospects. It is possible in fact, that the US "empire" has already peaked. For over 20 years now the US has been living beyond its means, borrowing heavily from the rest of the world to fund its activities (i.e. running large current account deficits). US consumption and other components of expenditure have grown faster than US income. The repatriation of profits from abroad is now being supplemented with borrowings from abroad to allow the government to run a large fiscal deficit as growing consumption (and necessarily, very low private savings) reduced the United States' ability to finance the fiscal deficit and private investment domestically.

Ongoing borrowing from abroad and sustained deficits have made the US a major net debtor. The broadest measure of the amount the US owes the rest of the world – the net international investment position (NIIP) – went from $360 billion in 1997 to $2.55 trillion at the end of 2005. In other words, the US owed the rest of the world $2.55 trillion (and this figure is rising). Ironically, perhaps, the largest portion of this dept is owed to China, which by comparison, is now a major net creditor. At then end of 2006, China was owed about $1.0 trillion by the rest of the world.

Writing in the Financial Times at the end of 2002, Harold James, professor of history at Princeton University and author of the book, *The End of Globalization*, suggested that, "one way of looking at this situation is that the rest of the world has bought into US stability. US deficits are financed by capital inflows, as the non-American world buys the stock of fast-growing US companies or - when the stock market looks bad - property. Indeed, there appears to be a security premium that the rest of the world pays, in that non-American purchases of US assets show consistently lower returns than US purchases of foreign assets."

But he continues, "Nobody really believes that this kind of inflow can be sustained indefinitely. Indeed, the inflows of foreign capital could be rapidly reversed on some chance piece of bad news. Such a reversal would involve a collapse of the US stock market, the property market, and the dollar. US consumers would no longer be able to binge on cheap goods supplied by the rest of the world... The financial reversal would also bring the collapse of US security policy. The cost of US defence spending would look much too high and scaling it down would give a chance to terrorists, enemies and would-be rivals to take the initiative. The situation of the US would then look more like that of 19th century Spain (which also ran a current account deficit, financed by the outflow of precious metals from its imperial possessions)," or, dare I say it, the collapsing Roman Empire.

And what chance piece of bad news might trigger such a series of events? Another September 11? A serious disruption of oil markets? A massive outflow of foreign capital to new, emerging markets, such as China or India? The chances of any or even all of these happening increases with every passing day.

Unless there is a rapid readjustment in lifestyles, expectations, politics, and economics in the US then somewhere down the road disaster is almost inevitable. History tells us that empires become too arrogant and self-obsessed to see the writing on the wall. Will things be any different this time?

It certainly seems as if the US administration has already become arrogant. It's response to September 11 demonstrated an administration that was not prepared to question its own actions and motives. Its mission seemed to be more concerned with enforcing the US view of the world, whether right or wrong, and to destroy anyone or anything that threatened that view. This is not the behaviour of a healthy, confident democratic country. This is the behaviour of a country that has lost the capacity for self-reflection. That has replaced confidence with arrogance. Nobody is always right, there is always something to learn and in a rapidly changing world there is always a need to review strategy and evolve to changing circumstances.

11. People power

For many decades now Western citizens have managed to live relatively privileged and "unaccountable" lives. We have been aware of certain problems in the world: famine and poverty in Africa; destruction of rain forests in South America; environmental pollution; climate change; terrorism and so on. However, we seem to have managed to turn a blind eye to the links between these problems and our own everyday lives. We have managed to convince ourselves that it is not our responsibility.

This, put simply, is self-delusion. In truth, we have very important responsibilities in relation to these matters and we have a moral obligation to accept these responsibilities. We, the citizens of the West have the financial and political power to change the course of the world. Our actions or inactions, or the actions or inactions of the leaders we elect are directly responsible for all of these issues and for bringing about the situation we find ourselves in today. Equally, it is such action or inaction that will determine how we deal with this situation. Make no mistake, there is nowhere else to turn, it is up to us.

But if it is up to us, then we really have to ask ourselves why we have failed so miserably to date? I believe there are a number of reasons for this. Firstly, I think there is ignorance. There is a lack of awareness and knowledge of global issues and a lack of appreciation of the global impact of our own actions. Secondly, I think we have managed to convince ourselves that we are not responsible. We have, mistakenly, come to believe that it's not up to us, that it's up to our governments and political leaders to sort out these problems.

And thirdly, I think there are those who consciously or subconsciously harbour concerns that any serious attempt to address these global issues could have a negative impact on their own lives. There is a hidden fear that a serious attempt to address global problems could involve financial or lifestyle sacrifices that people would prefer not to have to make.

The latter might seem like a very selfish and irresponsible attitude, but in a way it is not really surprising. We are human, and in the not too distant past our own ancestors often faced perilous and uncertain futures. The instinct to be competitive and to strive to maximise our own wealth and resources and that of our direct community is deeply ingrained in all of us.

However, this instinct is somewhat misplaced in today's world. For a start, levels of wealth in the West are such that we have now moved far beyond meeting our basic needs. As a community, we don't need to keep striving to become wealthier. We are now in the privileged position where we can take a wider perspective and look beyond our immediate survival. We can plan for the future, for our medium and longer term survival. This means planning for how we can better manage our natural resources, and how we can improve the welfare of the millions of people living poverty, thereby avoiding mass migration, conflict and other destabilising events.

And this does not necessarily have to be a major burden or sacrifice. If we act collectively, small sustained adjustments in behaviour could have an enormous impact. For example, by simply paying more attention to the products and services we buy we could have a significant impact on the environment without suffering any noticeable negative impact on our quality of life. Equally, reducing our consumption of unnecessary lifestyle items and increasing our contribution to developing countries we could effectively wipe out poverty overnight.

I work as a civil servant and my gross income is about €70,000 per annum. This is a little over twice the average industrial wage in Europe, but there are many people in the West on similar or higher salaries. If I were to be completely honest, I know that I could probably give away at least €500 of my salary every month without having to alter my lifestyle in any noticeable way. In fact, less than a year ago, before I started my current job, my salary was about €800 less per month and my lifestyle has not changed very much since.

If I can do this on my salary then what can we do as a society? Of course there are many who earn less than this, but there are also many who earn as much or more and quite a few who earn significantly more. If we were all to take a good look at our lives we would probably find that we could maintain a largely unaltered, and perfectly comfortable lifestyle on a lot less money.

If we consider for a moment that every person in the West who receives an income contributes, say, on average €125 per month (assuming some will pay less or nothing and some will pay more). If we were just to consider the US, Japan, Canada, Australia and the 15 wealthiest countries in the EU, which together have a combined workforce of around 400 million people, this would amount to about €50 billion per month, or €600 billion per year.

To put this in context, current worldwide development aid stands at around €50 billon per year and it would only require a doubling of this, to €100 billion to meet the amount required to achieve the Millennium Development Goals (the eight Millennium Development Goals range from halving extreme poverty to halting the spread of HIV/AIDS and providing universal primary education, all by the target date of 2015). One immediate impact achieving the Millennium Development Goal would be to save the lives of about 2 million children under 5 years of age every year. Meeting this target would require an average additional contribution of a mere €10.40 per month by the world's 400 million richest workers.

If these same workers could commit to and average additional contribution of €125 per month for a period of say three years, then the hopeless situation that currently exists in many developing countries would be transformed forever.

Would people sign up to such an initiative? Well, think about what €125 per month actually equates to (and remember, this is an average, most people would pay a lot less than this): a 15 cigarette per day smoking habit, a packed lunch instead of a sandwich at the deli, taking the bus to work instead of the car? We can all decide for ourselves whether or not we can afford this, or whether or not we are willing the make the necessary lifestyle changes to make it affordable, but my belief is that people would respond positively. I believe that humans are by nature caring. Just look at the response to the Tsunami disaster in Asia. I am quite certain that if we had a properly organised campaign, with a fixed timeframe and clear and realistic objectives then people would respond.

The benefits of such an initiative would also go beyond eradicating severe poverty. Taking €125 per month out of the pockets of the worlds biggest consumers could also be catalyst for the more profound changes that are also required in the Western lifestyle. Cutting back on our electricity use, cutting out unnecessary car journeys, better managing our household expenditure, reducing our waste collection bill, and perhaps substituting an overseas holiday with a break a little closer to home - all of these activities could help us to save to make up this €125, and perhaps even surpass it.

This wider lifestyle change is fundamental to achieving lasting change and to ensuring longterm sustainability. History has shown us that it's not enough to simply throw money at our problems and hope they will go away. They don't. In my view this has been a serious mistake in the past. While we have on occasion dug deep into our pockets and given generously, we have never made a real emotional or psychological connection with the causes to which we have given, we have never really examined the underlying problems and our role in creating these, and we have never made any serious attempt to address the root causes of these problems.

Neighbours

Imagine there is an immigrant family living on your street or in your neighbourhood and that they are in serious financial trouble. You don't know them very well as they only moved in about 6 months earlier and they speak very little English, but you are aware that the parents, who are not well educated, have found it impossible to find work and are finding it increasingly difficult to support their five young children. The family are receiving some State support but they are struggling to survive on this.

You are frequently reminded of the suffering of this family. As you drive your kids to school on a cold winter's mornings you see the kids begging on the street, dressed only in rags. You know they are cold and you suspect that they are probably also hungry. They are thin and sickly looking. Later in the day you see the mother begging in the local shopping centre and you often see the father collecting pieces of fire wood and other scraps from skips and rubbish piles along the street.

You don't intervene because you have been brought up to believe in a system that involves a pact between citizens and the State. The terms of this pact are that citizens pay their taxes to the State and the State in return provides for the needs of its citizens. So why, on top of paying your taxes, should you also start subsidising individual charity cases?

You raise this matter with your local politician who diplomatically explains to you that despite the fact that you pay your taxes, the taxes you pay are only sufficient to cover certain priority public services. To cover services outside of this, such as providing support to immigrants, people either have to pay more taxes or sacrifice cuts services in other areas.

You accept this explanation and you suggest to him that perhaps it is time to introduce a tax increase in order to raise money for immigrant support. He agrees and pledges to work towards this, if there is sufficient public demand in the future (secretly he is doubtful that this will ever happen, however).

In the meantime, the situation of the immigrant family continues to deteriorate and you know something has to be done immediately. You respond by raising the issue with family, friends and neighbours. To you surprise some of them give you money to give to the family and other promise to provide employment and other forms of assistance (food, childcare, language lessons, etc.). This support and assistance alleviates the immediate plight of the family. Crucially, however, through your actions you also succeed in raising awareness of the plight of immigrant families in your neighbourhood and at the next elections this issue is highlighted on the doorsteps. Following the elections the local Council sets up a new programme for immigrant families funded from a modest hike in local property tax.

This is a credible situation and an equally credible outcome and it perfectly demonstrates how at local level we can successfully exploit our powers as voters and economic entities to exert influence. Surely if we can exercise these powers at local level we can also do it at global level? And why do we have to wait until people from Africa or other developing countries are living next door to us before we offer assistance? Why can't we act now and, recognise their problems and help them to build a viable future in their own countries?

12. A new democracy

Today, in most Western countries ordinary people are losing interest in politics. This is clearly evident from the declining numbers turning out for elections. In many Western countries, including the US, upwards of 50% of the eligible population do not vote, which means that governments are governing without the active participation of over half the population..

This is not a healthy situation. A system of democratic governance that does not actively engage with half of its citizens is, in my view, stretching the definition of democracy. In fact, over time, such a system will tend to favour the interests of those who do engage, which are often the business and professional classes, serving to further alienate those who don't vote.

While there are many theories as to why voter turnout is in decline, in my view there is one overriding reason - most people believe that their participation will not make any difference. They don't perceive any real difference between the main political parties and, therefore, they don't believe that a change in government would make much difference. Most mainstream political parties now occupy the middle ground (centre right or centre left) and the general feeling is that no matter who people vote for life goes on pretty much unchanged. People don't really see politics as being able to change their lives for the better. They see it as something that can only have a marginal impact.

Most of the world's modern democracies have now reached this kind of equilibrium state, where things don't change much from one election to the next and where politics is really more about posturing and playing around at the fringes than effecting real change.

In all democracies there are competing interests. Supporters of the Welfare State invariably compete with the business community and free marketeers, industrialists compete with environmentalists, urban interests compete with rural interests, etc. But somewhere in all of this a balance is found, a sort of compromise is forged. Most mature democracies have reached this point and therefore, beyond slight adjustments or corrections from time to time, governments tend to work to preserve this balance. Radical change is rarely if ever on the agenda and therefore people don't view politics as a means of achieving change.

If you are ill, you will not be interested in waiting until the next general election to be saved by the promise of an increase in expenditure on healthcare. If you are unemployed you will not be pinning all you're hopes of getting a job on the opposition party's promise of a new employment scheme. Or if your business is going down the tubes, a change in government from the centre left to the centre right is unlikely to save the day. Governance is now essentially about small incremental changes of policy and this does not excite voters.

In this context, successful politicians tend to be people who can maintain the status quo while introducing, at most, minor and non-controversial reforms. They do not take political risks and they are rarely visionaries or leaders. They are managers.

A further contributory factor to the declining interest in politics is the increasing focus on the individual. In recent decades the power of the State has been greatly reduced as the focus on the role of the individual has taken on greater importance. The trend of governance has been for the State to interfere less and less, leaving the provision of more and more products and services to the free market. Deregulation and competition have become the order of the day, with the State even opting to reduce its role in such areas as healthcare, public transport, and education, thereby allowing for tax reductions, and giving the individual more disposable income and more control of where he or she purchases these services on the open market.

In this situation, individuals have much more control over, and responsibility for their own destiny and are less likely to look to the State to solve their problems. People therefore tend to devote less time to politics and governance and more time to looking after their own affairs, which creates less interdependence in society and a greater sense of self reliance.

On top of all this, the vast majority of people in the West are now reasonably well-off, lead relatively comfortable lives and don't feel there is much they want to change. For much of the history of democratic governance the aspiration has mostly been about improving standards of living, or, to put it another way, economic growth. Governments have, and with good reason, largely been judged on how they have managed the economy and how they have contributed to improving standards of living.

However, in recent decades most Western countries have reached a relatively high standard of living. We have accepted that our governments have been generally successful at giving us a better standard of living and we don't really believe that they are now going to mess it up. As a result we have become "passive democrats." In many ways an unwritten pact has been agreed between States and their citizens: the State has given us more and more control and responsibility over our own lives and in return we have allowed our governments to get on with their job with less interference.

But we now live in a new world and the parameters have changed, significantly. The days of the economy being the only important issue are gone. Increasingly, it is recognised that a successful and sustainable society must find a better balance between economic, environmental and social concerns and cannot focus on one at the expense of the others. Furthermore, we now live in a global society, and while the Western economy might be successful, there are many other regions of the world where economic development is still in its infancy.

In this context, the belief that politics cannot effect real radical change in our lives is no longer valid. Combating climate change, ending poverty and removing the underlying causes of global conflict are major challenges that have huge implications for all of us. Politics has a central role to play in addressing these issues.

We have an enormous opportunity now to reengage with the democratic process, but in a different way this time. This time, we need to think global. We need to look at setting new and ambitions challenges for our governments. But in future, we need to look outside of our own domestic and self-interest to identify these challenges.

We have come to associate politics and government with our immediate needs and our own immediate environment. We need to change this. We need to look at politics and governance in terms of the wider world. If we look outside of our own immediate environment there are many serious issues to be addressed and our governments have an important role to play in addressing these and we must encourage and mandate them to do so.

Given the state of the world we now live in we cannot afford to be apolitical. We cannot afford to disengage from the political process. We urgently need to reclaim our political powers and use them to goof effect. We need to highlight the serious issues that we want our political leaders to address - issues like climate change, poverty in developing countries, and relations with countries in the Middle East - and we need to elect those who we feel will best address these issues. This is an opportunity for us to get excited again about politics and about reasserting the democratic principles for which our ancestors fought and died.

13. Losing our religion

As with politics, it is evident that many people are now also disengaging from religion. In ever greater numbers people are coming to the conclusion that religion has little meaning or relevance to their lives.

Regrettably, the options open to those of us in this situation are limited, with the result that the spiritual side of our lives often gets ignored, leaving a void or a gap. It is not uncommon for people to look to materialism to fill this void and, in a way, this has become a modern day religion (for the millions of people for whom Sunday is now a day of shopping rather than a day of worship, with the huge shopping malls that have sprung up around our towns and cities becoming our modern day temples).

Ultimately, however, materialism does not provide spiritual fulfilment. Materialism is something that keeps us busy and helps us, temporarily, to forget our deeper needs. It offers only the promise of fulfilment, but not fulfilment itself.

Despite this, many of us get caught up in a vicious cycle of materialism and we find it difficult to escape because it becomes our life. We begin to live for our materialistic possessions and to focus all our time and energy on acquiring them. The irony of this situation is that many of us know how empty and futile this is but still we find it almost impossible to stop. Somehow, it feels as if it is out of our control, that we are part of a materialistic system and that there are no alternatives.

This is not actually the case, however. I have now come to realise that there is an alternative, that will not only allow us to unburden ourselves of our materialistic shackles, but at the same time will help us to rediscover our own inner spirituality and with it a whole new outlook on life.

If we look back to the origins of religion we can remind ourselves of some of the fundamentals of religion and spirituality, which, over time, have become clouded in the politics and bureaucracy of religious movements.

Religion originally developed as a means of explaining the unknowns in the world. How did we get here? What happens when we die? Who charts the course of our lives? And why did this years harvest fail? It served to unite people around certain belief systems that attempted to answer these questions in a coherent manner.

But religion also had a much more practical purpose. It also served to bring a certain order and stability to society, largely through the rules or rituals which gave expression to religious beliefs in ones everyday life. Historically, therefore, religion played an important role in shaping our behaviour and in determining how we relate to other people and to the world around us.

Of course the rules and rituals that govern our lives do not depend solely on our religious beliefs. As human beings we are innately spiritual and by educating our conscience we enable this sense of inner spirituality to guide our own personal actions. This education of our conscience is essential to our growth and maturity and is a life-long process which takes place through the influence of, and personal reflection on experience.

A moral way of life can therefore be taught, by informing the conscience through education, public debate and discussion, and by our actions and experiences. Religion traditionally played a very important part in this process. But there is a view, which I share, that religion as we know it today has lost this capacity. Rather than nurturing the development of the conscience and thereby giving us the freedom, and responsibility to develop our own private moral integrity, religions today often seek to impose rules and beliefs that are outdated and do not reflect the realities of the world in which we now live.

As religion has become more bureaucratic and more dictatorial, its role in nurturing this personal journey of spiritual discovery and of finding ones own moral code has been replaced by the imposition of a strict and narrowly defined dogma.

Such prescribed beliefs sometimes contradict what our conscience is telling us (for example, not all Catholics agree with the position of the Catholic Church on the use of condoms to prevent the spread of AIDS, or on issues such as divorce or abortion). This has lead many people to question their religious beliefs and increasing numbers, particularly in the West, to cease practising their religion.

I am one of these people. As I grew up and had the benefit of education and experience I found that my religion lost relevance. It proscribed a moral framework that I found to be static and not relevant to the world I knew. Effectively, I felt excluded from my religion because I had developed my own sense of right and wrong, which I found was not always compatible with the teachings of my religion. Despite its claims to being all embracing, fundamentally, I found my religion, like many others, to be intolerant, inflexible and judgemental. It had become preoccupied with rules and ritual and in my view it had lost sight of what was truly important – guiding ordinary people, like me, on our own personal journey of educating our conscience. To me, it didn't matter if a Catholic priest was married or not, or if he ate fish on a Friday, as long as he provided guidance and leadership on how to lead a moral and principled life and assisted the members of his congregation to do likewise. Most Catholics I know feel the same about these outdated rules and regulations.

In my view, these rules serve only to corrupt the Catholic church (for example, the many cases of Catholic priests found to be having sexual relationships with women, men, and even young boys), alienate the congregation and, ultimately, to divert attention away from the important issues that confront us today.

Religion has not always been like this, however. In the beginning, religious teaching focussed on connection rather than correction, based on the view that when the connections (between people) grow strong, so too does the desire to do the right thing. It therefore focused on strengthening connection and nurturing personal spiritual discovery rather than setting strict dogmas.

I was disappointed that my religion seemed to have abandoned this philosophy, leaving me and many others like me with little choice but to develop and nurture our own morals and spirituality in an increasingly complex world.

This has presented us with an enormous challenge. Rediscovering our own sense of spirituality and reawakening the growth and development of our conscience is not something that just happens. It requires effort and lifelong commitment. It is also not something that can do alone. To understand our own place in the world we also need to better understand the world around us. We need to understand our relationship with people and things and the consequences and impact of our thoughts and actions. We need to connect.

Religion once facilitated this process and perhaps it will again in the future. In the meantime, however, with no moral and spiritual compass, many of us spend our lives searching (mostly not knowing what we are searching for, but sometimes, hopelessly, trying to find it in materialism) and, invariably, losing sight of what is most important.

But perhaps this search is less complicated that we might imagine. Mostly we see ourselves as human beings in search of spirituality, a sometimes nebulous and intangible concept. But what if we turn this around and consider ourselves instead as spiritual beings in search of human experiences. Now, rather than seeking spirituality, we simply need to nurture it thorough our experiences. This is a very different proposition, as now our search focuses on knowledge and human experience instead of spirituality, which is a much easier concept to grasp.

Religion has traditionally played a role in helping to make the link between human experience and spirituality, but other institutions can also fulfil this role, and possibly more successfully. The important thing is the human experience and how we use this experience to nurture and develop our spirituality.

When spirituality becomes part of our daily experiences like this, the language that aims to describe it is also likely to appear less abstract and it should, therefore, become easier to intellectually connect spirituality with morality and to view it as separate from religion.

Spiritual development can be a powerful force in society. While political systems might establish laws and regulations that seek to shape and control our behaviour, ultimately, society, including its laws and regulations, is shaped by our collective conscience. It is crucial in today's society, therefore, that we educate our conscience about the global world in which we now live.

It is crucial, for example, that we educate ourselves about the AIDS pandemic in Africa if we are to allow ourselves to be guided on what this means for our own actions and decisions. We could decide to continue to ignore such issues, to continue to avoid this human experience. But in doing this we thwart our own spiritual development and our own growth and maturity as spiritual beings.

To grow and develop and to achieve spiritual fulfilment we need to embrace human experience. We need to seek to better understand the world we live in and our role therein.

This is not always easy in the modern world, where our time and energy is sapped by our 24/7 lifestyles. But it is something I believe we need to rethink. Principally, I believe we need to rejuvenate the idea of a day of reflection. The Sabbath was traditionally a day of prayer and reflection, a day to take stock of our lives and to reflect on how we interact with the world around us. It is regretful, therefore, that in its present incarnation the Sabbath is for many little more than a day to “go through the motions” of religious ritual and ceremony, or even worse, to go shopping.

It is unfortunate that for a growing number of people the Sabbath is no longer a day to stop and reflect, and therefore, that people are missing the opportunity to nurture their own spiritual development.

Given the serious global challenges we now face, I believe that rediscovering the true meaning of the Sabbath could present us with a wonderful opportunity to reflect and educate ourselves on the problems of the world and to consider ways in which we can respond to theses problems in our own lives and in our own communities.

Such a day of reflection does not necessarily have to be linked to religion, but for those who are religious, it could present an opportunity to rediscover the true meaning of the Sabbath and to reflect on what their religious teachings actually mean to people in their present day lives. It seems a terrible shame that religions do not use the Sabbath to be more proactive in helping to better make the connection between their fundamental teachings and the daily lives and responsibilities of their congregation (to their fellow man and to the environment, for example).

For those who are not religious, I believe the idea of a day of reflection could present an opportunity to consider their own individual beliefs and to reflect on their own place in the world and the responsibilities that this brings. This day could be Sunday, which for many is a day when they do not work. But equally it could be any day during which one could devote time to reflect on life's bigger issues. This could be a time to privately reflect on one's morality and on one's role in the wider world. Or it could be an opportunity to come together with members of the local communities, or with family and/or friends to "connect" and to collectively reflect on issues in society, on individual and shared beliefs, and to identify ways in which individually and collectively they could take action to address these issues.

"Today we may say aloud before an awe-struck world: 'We are still masters of our fate. We are still captain of our souls." *Sir Winston Churchill.*

14. World Party

Having spent over four years considering the current state of the world I have come to the conclusion that to successfully address the serious global issues that now confront us, and put the world on amore sustainable trajectory, we need to establish a new "bottom up" or people driven global initiative and a new sense of global citizenship. We need to create a new initiative that transcends race, religion or creed and that can give guidance and inspiration to people across the globe who care about the future of the planet and are willing to take action.

Ordinary people across the world could be invited to join or become members of this new initiative, which I provisionally call the World Party. I use the term World Party because I believe that it not only describes the coming together of people (party) at a global level (world) but it also creates a sense of hope or celebration (party) in the fact that we can work together to create a new and exciting world in our own lifetime. I think it is important that we focus on the very positive impact that we can have on the world if we make this effort.

World Party is a simple concept. It is effectively about citizens collectively taking responsibility for their own actions. It's about people taking responsibility for using their power as consumers, as voters and as economic entities and it is about people working together to ensure that this power has global impact. World Party is also about people, including parents, who are interested in acting now to ensure that our children and grandchildren inherit a planet that is alive and healthy and not one on the verge of collapse.

The World Party concept takes account of the fact that the world is now a very complex place, where there is extensive global interaction and rapid technological and social development. This new global environment has resulted in a radical transformation in many aspects of our lives, such as trade, travel, communications, culture, but it has not been accompanied by the same transformation in social, religious or political systems, or in how we view ourselves as citizens.

Because of this many people are ignorant or confused about their responsibilities in the wider world: about their role in protecting the global environment; their role in helping those living in poverty in developing countries; or their role in resolving wars and conflicts. When we consider the natural environment we are unsure as to what our individual responsibilities are: what should we be doing to promote environmental protection? Should we leave our car at home and walk to work? Should we get a smaller, more efficient car? What goods and services should we buy and what should we not buy? Will it make any difference? And how do we know when we are doing enough?

We do know, or should know, that it is morally wrong to knowingly harm the environment in any way. But do we feel any moral responsibility for the damage that is being done to the environment because of what we do: the goods we buy, the cars we drive, the houses we build? And if we do, what do we do about it?

Similarly, we all know it would be morally wrong for us to stand by without giving food or money if our neighbour was dying from starvation. But do we accept any responsibility for standing by while millions of our fellow human beings in developing countries live in abject poverty and die in their thousands every day from hunger and disease?

To move forward as a race we must address these questions, individually and collectively. It is imperative that we begin to exercise our responsibilities as citizens and our powers as voters and consumers to bring about positive change in the world. This is our responsibility to our fellow human beings and, crucially, to our children and future generations.

World Party is about the coming together of people with shared concerns and a shared commitment to work together to create a better world for themselves and their children. They key aspects of the World Party concept include:

1. A global initiative to establish a mechanism to facilitate people to alter their behaviour, focusing on a shift towards more sustainable lifestyles, greater human solidarity, and a more peaceful and secure society.

2. An initiative that aims to mobilise people across the globe to establish local World Party (WP) groups (groups members could be family members, friends, neighbours, colleagues, people from the same church, etc.) which would have two objectives:
    a. To educate their members about global issues, in particular environmental, development, and security issues.
    b. Arising from this, to facilitate members in taking action in their own lives and in their locality that would

contribute to addressing these issues (for example, reduce car use, greater energy efficiency, increase pressure for government action, support and assistance to developing countries, ethical shopping and investing)

3. The network of local WP Groups around the world would be supported by National and International Support Units and a Global Support Unit. These units would be established and funded by existing national and international organisations (governments, charities, NGO's, United Nations, for example) and their function would be to provide coordination and to give expert advice and direction to the local WP Groups (on actions and initiatives that they could take at local level, for example). The support units would also gather information on the WP groups and their work which they would use to monitor the progress of the initiative and to facilitate the exchange of ideas and good practices. The support units would benefit from input from an international forum of experts and civil leaders. The collective actions of the WP groups, supported and directed by National, International and a Global Support Unit would ensure global impact (and thereby ensure that people do not feel they're wasting their time).

4. In order to engender support and to motivate participations to actively participate in something that requires change and commitment the WP initiative would have an initial timeframe of three years. At the end of three years it would be reviewed and its impact evaluated. It is expected that the initiative will have a major impact in just three years, particularly in relation to carbon emissions (climate change) and poverty. However, it is also

expected that by then, participants will have become accustomed to a new and different way of life and that the opportunity will exist to establish a more permanent initiative.

5. Launching the WP initiative would require the support and assistance of a wide range of national and international organisations that have reach and influence in society (churches, political groups, NGO's, schools, and sports groups, for example). The initiative would also seek leadership from well-known personalities in the world of music, TV and film, sports, politics, etc.

6. The WP initiative is about people taking responsibility for creating a better future for themselves and for their children and future generations. Its success will require the leadership of individuals to kick-start WP at all levels: local, national, international, and global, including the establishment of the Forum. Such leaders already exist at all of these levels.

The World Party concept provides a mechanism to ensure that public interest in global issues - aroused sometimes by global disasters, or organised global campaigns – is sustained and translated into individual responsibility and action. It facilitates a structured and coordinated response to a range of global issues, such as the environmental, development, and global conflict, providing a real opportunity to mobilise people across the planet to engage in a single project that aims to change the world.

At local level people could decide to be individual members and work independently or they could decide to become part of a local WP group. Some level of engagement at group level is desirable, however, as the exchange of views, experiences, and learning that occurs in groups, and the impact of joint action, cannot be achieved by people working only independently.

Local WP groups could be formed by anyone and could be of any size. I do not believe that there should be any rituals or ceremony associated with WP groups, or that there needs to be any formal approach. I believe people should organise themselves as they see fit, or as they might for any other project in their community.

For example, a group could be formed by a small group of friends and family or it could be a group of colleagues, or people from a particular neighbourhood. It could also be an existing group, which has been established for another purpose but that decides to take on this added dimension. It would also be desirable for existing religious groups to embrace this concept.

Depending on the number and the profile of members, a group could meet in the town hall, a local community centre, in their local pub, in the house of a friend or family member, or really wherever they find it most convenient.

Local WP Group Structure

While I don't believe that local WP groups should have any formal or rigid structure, there are certain basic requirements to ensure the effective working of any group. Firstly, each meeting should ideally be facilitated (chaired) by a group member. This could be done on a rotation basis, with a different member chairing each meeting, or the group members could decide that they want to appoint a chairperson for a longer period. In the case of the latter, I would seriously suggest that this period is not longer than 6 months to ensure that the group builds capacity and does not become preoccupied with the agenda or interests of any one person.

Beyond this the members could decide how formal or informal they would like their groups to become.

I believe meetings should be held once per week, but this is completely up to the groups themselves (groups, or indeed individuals, should decide on their own day of reflection or "sabbath" and may decide to meet more than once per week). Given that it is not a working day in many western countries, perhaps Sunday would be a good time, but again this is completely up to the group members.

Local WP Group Objectives

The main objectives of the local WP groups would be: 1. to enhance members' understanding of key global issues and strategies to address these issues; and 2. to plan and implement actions at local level as part of a coordinated global initiative to address these issues. The regular local WP group meetings would, therefore, aim to facilitate the following:

1. Education

   To inform and educate the members of the group on key global issues, on the strategies being proposed to address these issues, and on the local dimension of the both the problems and the proposed solutions.

2. Discussion

   To facilitate discussion on these issues with a view to promoting enhanced understanding and ownership, and to help identify ways of altering behaviour or initiating action at local level.

3. Setting Objectives

On the basis of discussion and debate, and taking account of global WP priorities, to identify priority objectives on which members, either individually and/or as a group, would focus.

4. Guidance / Advice

   With input from the appropriate International and National Support Units, provide guidance and advice to the members on what they can do, as individuals and as a group, to help achieve these priority objectives.

5. Planning

   To facilitate the planning of activities to be undertaken by the group and/or by individual members in order to achieve the identified objectives of the group. Planning would also draw on the expert advice and guidance available from the relevant National, International and Global Support Units.

6. Implementation

   Outside of meetings the members, either individually and/or as a group, would engage in the implementation of their group's plans and initiatives. This might involve changing certain aspects of how they live their lives, like using their car less. It might also include specific projects which they undertake collectively or individually, such as establishing links with charities, or setting up a community based recycling or renewable energy project.

7. Support

   To support this ongoing work, the group would continuously review its own activities and, where relevant, would inform the members of new developments which might impact on these activities, thereby facilitating expert input into the ongoing work of the group.

Local Group Activities

Local group activities should focus on making a local contribution to addressing global issues, particularly in the areas of the environment, addressing social injustice and inequality (particularly in developing countries), and global conflict.

For example, in the area of the environment possible activities might include: informing members of environmental issues, and in particular climate change and the local factors that contribute to it and the local activities that could help to alleviate it; encouraging members to alter aspects of their lives which have a negative impact on climate change and the global environment generally (e.g. to commit to reduce their car use, to alter their consumption patterns, reduce energy consumption, reduce air travel, and preserve green space for example) and to undertake actions which have a positive environmental impact (planting of trees and development of green areas, increase use of renewable energy, purchase local good and services where possible, for example).

Emissions from motorised vehicles are known to be one of the biggest contributors to the processes causing climate change. Local groups could also look at starting initiatives to reduce their contribution to this problem. This might include: promoting the purchase of "green" cars (hybrids or cars using biofuels, for example); encouraging people to use their car less by promoting walking, cycling, and improved public or community transport; encouraging people to fly less, perhaps by holidaying more at home or if they go abroad, to take the train or ferry where possible;

and generally encouraging people to consider how they can reduce emissions from motorised vehicles. As an initial target, members could seek to halve their overall emissions.

In relation to addressing global poverty and inequality the emphasis could initially be on providing resources. Local group members could look at their financial situation and establish an ongoing contribution that they feel they can afford (significant weekly, monthly or annual payment) to a group fund. How this money is used should be decided by the group members. However, money could be collected by the National or International Support Units for large scale projects. In such circumstances every effort should be made to ensure that the minimum amount necessary is used for administration or other associated expenditure.

In deciding how to use their funds, groups should, where possible, aim to make a psychological as a well as a financial investment. There should be a serious attempt to identify how best this money can best be used, where and to whom it should go and what other supports (skills, expertise, etc.) could also be provided that would add value to any financial assistance.

For example, a local group could work with some of the existing and reputable charity organisation to try to identify specific projects or communities in developing countries that could be assisted on an ongoing basis. Groups could consider the full range of supports and assistance that they could provide, be it financial, expertise, training, etc and try to match this to the project/community that they could assist. Local groups could also cooperate among themselves for certain aspects of this work. For example, if a group wanted to help an entire village community in a developing country then they could look at working with other local WP groups so that they would have access to more resources and a wider range of relevant skills.

In the area of conflict and international terrorism, each local group should make an effort to learn more about the underlying causes of conflict and about the cultural and political traditions of the parties involved. This could include an ongoing education programme to enhance understanding and appreciation of different cultures and beliefs. This might, for example, include the exchange of speakers between different communities – Palestinian local group members speaking to Jewish local group members; Americans and British speaking to Middle Eastern Muslims; or Northern Irish Protestants speaking to Northern Irish Catholics.

Local groups could also look at the causes of conflict and could work to ensure that they are not contributing in any way, such as, by supporting, directly or indirectly, corporations or governments that are exploiting other regions of the world and thereby creating the conditions for conflict.

In all areas of activity local groups should consider how they can use their economic and political power to bring about positive change. What should they purchase and what should they try not to purchase (i.e. what are the non-ethical goods and services)? How could they positively influence their govenments? What should their key considerations be at election time? Local WP group members should be mindful of the importance of their actions for their children, grandchildren, and future generations.

It is important that each local group works at a pace that is acceptable to its members. Members should not be lost because they feel they cannot keep up with the activities of the group. Members should be allowed to work at their own pace, and within their own resource capability and this must be fully respected by the other group members.

It would not be constructive to advocate that people immediately stop driving their car so as to avoid contributing to global warming, or that they give all their savings to charity. Everyone has grown up with the expectation of a certain standard of living and the aim should not be to make life intolerable for these people by drastically reducing their quality of life.

This would be unfair and unrealistic and, in the long term people would not respond positively to such an approach.

The aim instead should be to facilitate people to move over time to a lifestyle that is sustainable for all the inhabitants of the world.

The motivation for this initiative should come from our own knowledge and understanding of the fact that we are now living in a world where the environment is damaged and deteriorating and where there is growing tensions and inequality between the small number of people who control, and enjoy the benefits of most of the earth's limited resources, and the growing numbers of the world's poor. Is this the world we want to live in, or is this the world we want our children to inherit? And if not, what are we willing to do about it?

The local WP groups will be the powerhouses of the WP concept. In some bigger countries, or countries with well developed regional structures, then perhaps regional support structures, similar to that proposed below for the national level, might also be appropriate at regional level.

The WP concept does, however, require ***National Support Units*** to facilitate and support the work of the local groups. Such Units could facilitate access to expert advice and assistance in order to guide the work of the local groups. This might include information on international research or studies, or updates on political developments, or it might also include facilitating access to experts who could visit groups as guest speakers to discuss certain issues. The National Support Units would also facilitate networking between groups, which could allow for groups to exchange best practice or even to cooperate and undertake joint projects.

The WP National Support Units could be hosted by government bodies or by Non Governmental Organisations (NGOs) which have the resources to establish and run such a service at national level. An important aspect of this national support service would be a WP national website, which would facilitate access to information, databases of experts, networking and information on best practice, and other WP tools and information. The national WP Support Units could also organise regular events (seminars, conferences, etc.) to support the work of the local groups.

I would also propose that there should be International Support Units (or WP Observatories), with functions similar to that of the National Support Units. These could be run by international bodies (such as the European Union or other bodies that promote cooperation between countries), but there should also be one global support unit covering the entire globe and run by a global organisation, such as the United Nations.

The International Support Units would facilitate and support the work of the local WP groups by facilitating and supporting the work of the National Support Units within their geographical area of coverage. This work would include identifying and disseminating expert information (the latest research findings, for example) to help guide the action of local groups and also identifying and disseminating best practice. With the Global Support Unit, the International Support Units would also focus on ensuring efforts at national and local level are coordinated and focused on delivering maximum global impact.

World Party Advisory Group

To provide expert input into the work of local groups I would suggest that the Global Support Unit establishes a World Party Advisory Group, made up of people with no vested interests and people with international reputations for integrity and fairness, but also with the expertise and intellectual ability to present solutions to global problems to local WP groups. These solutions could then be disseminated by the support units to the local groups.

The activities of the Advisory Group would include engaging with the scientific community, governments, the academic world, international charities, industry, NGO's, etc. in order to analyse and find the best solutions that currently exist to international problems. All the work of the Group should be available for international scrutiny (complete transparency) and the conclusions of this work should be communicated to the local members of the World Party in a simple and concise manner which will allow people to understand what action is being recommended at local level.

The Advisory Group could initially focus on the priority issues: climate change, alleviating poverty in developing countries, and global peace and security and its membership should include representatives of organisations working in these key areas. It should also aim to have a good gender and geographical balance.

The success of the Advisory Group will depend largely on its integrity, which should never be compromised. A panel of potential members should be submitted by governments from around the world and the members could then be selected by intergovernmental agreement. I believe that a properly functioning Advisory Group, once established, could be self sustaining, appointing its own replacements, based on agreed and transparent rules.

15. A revolution

The publication in 1972 of *The Limits to Growth* (Meadows at al 1972) was a key event in terms of evolving perceptions of the concept of global sustainability. On the basis of a number of simulations using a computer model of the world system (World3), the authors of this seminal publication concluded that:

1. If the present growth trends in world population, industrialisation, pollution, food production and resource depletion continue unchanged, the limits to growth on this planet will be reached sometime in the next 100 years. The most probable result will be a sudden and uncontrollable decline in both population and industrial capacity.
2. It is possible to alter these trends and to establish a condition of ecological and economic stability that is sustainable far into the future. The state of global equilibrium could be designed so that the basic material needs of each person on earth are satisfied and each person has an equal opportunity to realise his or her individual human potential.

3. If the world's people decide to strive for this second outcome rather than the first, the sooner they begin working to attain it, the greater will be their chances of success.

A sequel to *The Limits to Growth*, written by the same team and entitled *Beyond the Limits*, was published in 1992. In this, the authors conclusion were as follows: "As far as we can tell from the global data, from the World3 model, and from all we have learned in the past twenty years, the three conclusion we drew in *The Limits to Growth* are still valid, but they need to be strengthened."

Every day we wait, 30,000 children die needlessly, between 100 and 150 plant and animal special become extinct forever, we lose 70,000 hectares of rainforest, we release another 150 million tonnes of Carbon Dioxide into the atmosphere, and another $3.0 billion is spent on arms and weapons of mass destruction. Every day we wait our chances of success deteriorate.

Up to now, we have been waiting from someone else to take the lead, waiting for governments or for corporations to guide the way. But now, we can no longer afford to do this. We need to act.

The World Party concept gives us this possibility. It is a "bottom up" approach which provides a mechanism for ordinary citizens to take the lead. Working together through a single global initiative, ordinary people have the power to:

- Bring about a fundamental cultural shift in the developed world, from a high consuming, high environmental impact, materialistic society to a lower consuming, low environmental impact, sustainable society, which is united around a new progressive and positive approach to the development of the planet.

- Forge a new collective agreement between the citizens of developed countries to seriously increase the allocation of resources (financial, human, technological, etc.) to eradicate poverty and suffering in the poorer regions of the world.

- Establish a new global agreement on how to address climate change.

- Facilitate the large scale introduction of new incentives (such as guaranteed prices) and supports (such as grant aid and improved grid access) to facilitate the speedy development of the renewable energy sector

- Put an end to the destruction of rainforests and biodiversity.

- Through global citizen action, promote peace and security to all areas of conflict.

Action in all of these areas requires international cooperation and solidarity and there must be a critical mass of support from all countries. Citizens across the globe need to commit to working together.

If we can achieve this, the prize is potentially enormous: to remove the shackles of materialism; to create a cleaner, greener environment; to establish global peace and stability; to eradicate poverty; and crucially, to build a more hopeful and sustainable future for our children and grandchildren.

We are fortunate in that we now have a choice. We can wait and allow things to get worse, or we can act now and try to seize this wonderful opportunity to change the course of our civilisation forever. If we wait we will only see a further deterioration in the environment, security, poverty and in international relations. Eventually it will reach a point where the damage is irreversible. If we act now we have a wonderful chance of succeeding and entering a new and exciting period in the development of the human race.

Our parents and grandparents' generations sacrificed their lives in two great wars to secure the freedom and independence that we enjoy today. Now it is our turn. This is our Great War, our World War III. This is our opportunity to advance a new vision of the world for our children and grandchildren and future generations. World War III does not have to be fought on battlefields. It can be fought in the hearts and minds of people across the globe. It does not have to be a war that divides; it can be a war that unites people across the globe in a battle to defeat poverty, environmental destruction, and global conflict.

> *"We know the problems. A child in Africa dies every three seconds from famine, disease or conflict. We know that if climate change is not stopped, all parts of the world will suffer. Some will even be destroyed, and we know the solution – sustainable development."* Prime Minister Tony Blair, speaking to the World Summit on Sustainable Development in Johannesburg in 2002.

www.ingramcontent.com/pod-product-compliance
Ingram Content Group UK Ltd.
Pitfield, Milton Keynes, MK11 3LW, UK
UKHW012241240726
13966UKWH00003B/1211